Happy Eyes

Happy Eyes

Becoming All Things to All People

Ryan Tillman

Foreword by Dak Prescott

ConnectEDD Publishing
Hanover, Pennsylvania

Copyright © 2023 by Ryan Tillman

All rights reserved. No part of this publication may be reproduced, distributed, or transmitted in any form or by any means, including photocopying, recording, or other electronic or mechanical methods, without the prior written permission of the publisher, except in the case of brief quotations embodied in critical reviews and certain other noncommercial uses permitted by copyright law. For permission requests, contact the publisher at: info@connecteddpublishing.com

This publication is available at discount pricing when purchased in quantity for educational purposes, promotions, or fundraisers. For inquiries and details, contact the publisher at: info@connecteddpublishing.com

Published by ConnectEDD Publishing LLC
Hanover, PA
www.connecteddpublishing.com

Cover Design: Kheila Dunkerly

Happy Eyes by Ryan Tillman. —1st ed.
Paperback ISBN 979-8-9874184-4-4

Praise for *Happy Eyes*

Happy Eyes: Becoming All Things to All People is a transformative guide that will challenge your preconceived notions and inspire you to approach every interaction with an open heart and mind. Ryan's personal journey and his commitment to fostering positive change make this book a must-read for anyone seeking to make a difference in their own lives and the lives of those around them. Prepare to be moved and motivated to embrace the power of love, empathy, and respect in all your relationships.

—Michael Strahan | Hall of Famer and TV personality

Leo Tolstoy observed and stated that "everyone thinks of changing the world, but no one thinks of changing himself." Ryan Tillman is the exception to this observation; he is the embodiment of a true change agent. His convictions are underpinned by his faith in and understanding of God's edicts expressed through his written word. Ryan understands the nuance of human interaction and the interdependence of relationships. From his initial platform as a law enforcement officer, he has continued to develop his gift as a societal bridge builder. Referencing the Stair-Step model of the Hierarchy of Competence, developed by Martin Broadwell, Ryan's objective is to enhance our cultural and social competence to be our best, at whatever we do.

Happy Eyes will challenge you to rethink how you envision yourself. To have better lives, we must become greater in spirit and expand our outlook. Ryan Tillman is doing his part toward shaping a better world. Are you?

—Mark Mitchell | Consultant

Ryan truly embraced the lifestyle of "Becoming all things to all people" from the first day of his law enforcement career. Like the Apostle Paul, Ryan was chosen to take his message of change, understanding, and compassion to the masses. The most honorable trait Ryan brings with his message of being all things to all people is an unwillingness to compromise truth. Paul the Apostle took the message of Christ to the communities who hadn't heard of His love, goodness, grace, and mercy but he didn't compromise the truth because he knew, as does Ryan, that only the truth will set you free.

—Rodney Lombard | Retired Police Lieutenant

Ryan's work demonstrates courageous leadership willing to challenge tradition and stretch one's thinking. Furthermore, it serves as a powerful read and speaks to his respect for the humanity of others.

—Chief Joseph G. Paulino

Looking for a book that will change your perspective on life? Look no further than Ryan Tillman's *Happy Eyes*. This inspiring read is all about seeing the best in everyone, even those who may hold vastly different opinions or backgrounds than your own. Through personal stories and experiences in law enforcement and beyond, Tillman shows readers the power of empathy, respect, and love in developing meaningful relationships with those around us. Whether you're part of an organization, school, agency, or community, *Happy Eyes* can help you transform your world from the inside out. So why wait? Pick up a copy today and let Tillman's wisdom guide you towards a happier, more fulfilling existence.

—Shea Degan | Founder & President 88 *Tactical*

Ryan provides us a unique and helpful guide on how to co-exist in an increasingly diverse community through his first-hand point of view from law enforcement, community, and caring. Thank you for your kindness and willingness to help others.

—Vernon Irvin | CEO and Board-member

This book could not have come at a more critical time. Ryan Tillman is a gifted communicator who has been able to bring the timeless truth of empathy, intentionality, and the power of authentic relationships to this present generation, crying out for community and belonging. This book challenges our current state of cancel culture and begs us all to get out of our silos and shadows of judgment, fear, and unnecessary angst and into the light of empathy, curiosity, and calmness. These simple truths are community changing!

—Kern Oduro | Ph.D. Assistant Superintendent, Student Services

Every endeavor that Ryan Tillman takes on shows his heart, character, and personal convictions. His new book is a deeper dive into what drives Ryan and why we can all learn from his principled approach to life. I encourage everyone to read this book.

—Darren Goodman | Police Chief

Ryan Tillman is the definition of "you grow through what you go through." We can all learn from his resiliency, outlook, and ability to turn life's trials into valuable lessons. I am beyond excited for the world to receive their *Happy Eyes* by diving into this book and learning from the best.

—Anthony Johnson | Police Officer, Keynote Speaker and Influencer

Ryan Tillman has real-life law enforcement experience bridging the gap with the community. This book will provide enlightenment and challenge readers to consider seeing beyond oneself to find their own purpose in effecting change.

—Anthony Vega | Police Captain

Ryan Tillman has made a positive impact both in law enforcement and our communities. Through his book *Happy Eyes, Becoming All Things to All People*, I am excited for readers to learn how leading and living with love, empathy and respect will allow you to break down barriers and build relationships with those who don't look, think, or vote like you.

—Wes Simmons | Chief of Police

Ryan Tillman has been instrumental in building bridges between law enforcement and communities all over the nation. In his book, *Happy Eyes, Becoming All Things to All People*, Ryan shares his life experiences and connections with people. He has dedicated his life to building relationships by getting people to better understand each other. Ryan recognizes that Love, Empathy and Respect are key components to societal growth.

—Kevin Mensen | Deputy Chief

If you want to make the world a better place read *Happy Eyes*. Ryan Tillman is the epitome of optimism and positive change in the world. In this book he shares how you can become a force for good in the world as well.

—Bedros Keuilian | entrepreneur, author, inspirational speaker

Through his powerful message, Ryan Tillman offers a guiding light in a society shrouded by division. His insights encourage us to embrace empathy, bridge divides, and build bridges of understanding. *Happy Eyes: Becoming All Things to All People* is an extraordinary book that has the potential to positively impact not only our individual lives but also the lives of everyone we encounter. It serves as a rallying cry for unity and reminds us that true change begins from within. I wish there were more people like Ryan in this world!

—Constance Schwartz-Morini | Co-Founder SMAC Entertainment

The eyes are windows to the soul. This well-known phrase is based on Bible verses from Matthew 6:22-23, "The eye is the lamp of the body. If your eyes are healthy, your whole body will be full of light. But if your eyes are unhealthy, your whole body will be full of darkness." In *Happy Eyes*, Corporal Tillman phenomenally illustrates the importance of perspective and seeing people through a lens of light rather than darkness to build relationships and create connections. In one quote, Tillman emphasizes, "we often get so hung up on another person's viewpoints, values and lifestyle that we miss out on the actual human…" His sincerity, transparency, and transformational tone coupled with his faith and dedication to positive change is truly aspirational. *Happy Eyes* is a must-read for anyone who aspires to be a good human being by shining a healthy light in the dark and unhealthy places.

—Lynne B. Kennedy | Ph.D.

Officer Ryan Tillman is a man of impeccable character and integrity. This is brilliantly demonstrated in his writing. Ryan's approach towards life and the preservation of life is reminiscent of Dale Carnegie's groundbreaking work on "How to Win Friends and Influence People." Tillman's philosophy and way of living begs for comparison to the great philosopher and prophet Allan Watts.

—Terrence Dashon Howard | Actor

Happy Eyes: Becoming All Things to All People by Ryan Tillman is an intensely powerful, eye-opening treatise on the invaluable art of empathy and respect in our increasingly polarized society. Drawing on the biblical figure of Paul the Apostle as a model, Tillman's own metamorphosis from a staunch critic of law enforcement to a police officer serves as a compelling backdrop to the book's central narrative.

—Dr. Keyisha Holmes

Ryan Tillman's example epitomizes the saying "practice what you preach." In a world of division it is easy to get caught in the polarization. Ryan gives us examples of leadership based on biblical principles that are applicable beyond race, gender, economic background, political ideology, religious beliefs, or profession. His book provides understanding of yesterday and hope for tomorrow.

—Leon Ford, Activist

Ryan Tillman has been instrumental in the work the Faith Fight Finish Foundation by Dak Prescott does to bridge the gap between law enforcement, youth, and the communities they serve. We bonded when he started working with the foundation shortly after the George Floyd tragedy and he is, perhaps, one of the best people I have ever met. Ryan has a wonderful innate ability to look at both sides of any situation without bias and a genuine love for the world and for all people. This book shares a raw and honest look at the experiences that have made him who he is, and invites us all to embrace the power of love, empathy, and respect in our connections with others. Although we live in perhaps as divisive a society as there's ever been, Tillman offers a gentle and encouraging reminder of the humanity that connects us all. Both timely and timeless, these pages demonstrate the beauty of compassion and the power of kindness in molding a better tomorrow. The thought-provoking and inspiring messages shared in *Happy Eyes* will appeal to every reader and stay with them long after they've finished the book.

—Shannon Mabrey Rotenberg, Executive Director, just keep livin Foundation & Faith Fight Finish Foundation

Dedication

This book is dedicated to my late Father, Earl Tillman, and my late Father-in-Law, Edwin Ragay. These two men shaped me into the man I am today. The traits that are necessary for success in life, family, and business were possessed by them, thus their legacy lives on through the words of this book.

Most importantly, I would like to dedicate this book to my beautiful wife Kimberly who has seen the "Happy Eyes" in me from day one. Without her support, no one would know who Ryan Tillman is. Thank you, Honey, for always believing in me and being my right hand!

Table of Contents

Foreword xvii

Introduction 1

Chapter 1: A Bridge Between Us 5
    Your Mission, Should You Choose to Accept It 5
    Beyond the Funnel 7
    An Invitation 8
    The Impossible is Possible 9
    A Way Forward 11

Chapter 2: Why Connection Matters 13
    What It Takes to Win Someone Over 14
    Scary but Worth It 15
    A Well-Rounded Perspective 16
    The Simple Math of Opportunity 16
    One Percent 17
    All Things to All People 18
    The Price of Contention 19
    The Rewards of Connection (Spiritual) 20
    The Rewards of Connection (Personal) 20
    The Rewards of Connection (Tangible) 22
    Heart Check 22
    Meeting Others at Pivotal Moments 24

Chapter 3: It Starts with Love 27
   Why Love?. 29
   Making Pivotal Moments Go Right 32
   Leading with Love 33
   Dangers of Inauthenticity 35
   This is Going to Sound So Strange 36

Chapter 4: Leading with Empathy. 39
   Empathy is a Requirement, Not a Choice. 41
   Empathy Misunderstood. 42
   Meet Emotional Trauma with Emotion 43
   Hypocrisy vs. Human 44
   Take it to the Bank. 46
   Empathy Has to Care 48
   Organic Empathy Comes from Expanding Your Circle 50

Chapter 5: The Power of Respect 53
   Respect is Earned Not Given…Or is It?. 54
   Be the Lion 56
   Respect and Disrespect are Two Sides of the Same Price Tag. ... 58
   Is it an Attack on Me? 59
   How to Keep from Taking it Personally 60
   Leading with Respect is an Intentional Mindset 62
   Career Criminal 63

Chapter 6: Influence Is Relational 65
   Why Relationships Matter 67
   One More for the Good. 69
   Service Before Self 72
   The Domino Effect of Your Efforts Today 73
   The Difference We Make. 75

TABLE OF CONTENTS

Chapter 7: Transformation 77
    Transformation is an Inward-Out Process 79
    Get Comfortable Being Uncomfortable 80
    Transformation: From Self to Kingdom 82

Chapter 8: Your Legacy is Now 85
    Dig Deep 85
    Bigger than Anything–For Someone Else 86
    Every School Has a Name 87
    The Choice is Yours 89
    The Comeback 90

Afterword 93
About the Author 97
More from ConnectEDD Publishing 99

Foreword

My experience of love, empathy, and respect comes from being the youngest of three boys. My brothers are five and six years older than me, and I've always been so blessed to feel loved as their little brother.

Being the youngest also gave me an amazing perspective: I've always said empathy comes from education, and watching my brothers, my mom, and my dad taught me how to have empathy for others in all circumstances—and just how impactful that can be.

My big brothers also taught me about respect. They made me earn everything with the way I played, and they showed me that respect is a two-way street.

I am a Black Multiracial American; in my life I've been the only Black man in the room and the only white one many, many times. Those situations really bring what's possible with love, empathy, and respect into focus. Like my good friend Ryan says, it's the only way to bridge the gap between groups that are in conflict with one another. We may look different, be a different color, or come from a different background, but when we lead with love, hear someone's story, and learn who they are, their trials and tribulations might allow us to connect. We can respect and bring empathy for someone who has felt the same things we have.

My friendship with Ryan grew out of a shared love of people and a hope of bridging the gap between communities and law enforcement.

He was in town with his organization, *Breaking Barriers United*, and I had just made a million-dollar pledge toward better police training and to address systemic racism after the murder of George Floyd. Our desire for peace between the two groups, and safety and healing in our communities, formed an instant bond. I'm blessed to know him and to share that passion for making a difference.

Ryan is the best person I know to write about love, empathy, and respect. He walks through his own life with purpose, authentically making and becoming the change we, both want to see. He gives back to the youth. He breaks the stigma around law enforcement at every turn. He has recruited so many of his friends and brothers to do the same. Most importantly, his words—and this book—are an outgrowth of his actions. With Ryan, love, empathy, and respect always come first.

I'm honored to call Ryan my friend and thankful that we can partner together.

Dak Prescott
2022 NFL Walter Payton Man of the Year

Introduction

Adrian.

A few years ago, I was working as a school resource officer, and had the opportunity to be on the proactive side of policing. It also helped me forge bonds with a lot of the kids at my school. Often, I became their dad, their big brother, their friend. One of these kids was named Adrian.

Adrian was a kid with a good heart. It was so obvious that he wanted to do the right thing. Sadly, he came from a family that was in and out of jail. In fact, I'd already arrested his dad several times. Sometimes, Adrian and I would even talk about it. "I had to pick up your dad last night," I'd say.

"Oh, really?"

"Yep."

Meanwhile, all the other kids at school would wonder what we were talking about.

Adrian loved wearing hats, but he always got them taken away by administrators for wearing them at inappropriate times. He had an entrepreneurial streak that I admired, too. One day I suggested he start a hat business and make hats with the school logo on them so he would be operating within the school rules (only hats with school logos were allowed at this school).

"Oh, man, that's actually a pretty good idea," he said.

Fast forward to summertime, about a year after I started mentoring Adrian. School was out, and I returned to my regular duties as a patrol officer. I still spent a lot of time at the school because I loved it there so much. One day while I was there hanging out with the administrators, a call came in over my radio. There was unknown trouble in the neighborhood, and the responding officers needed help. Immediately.

I went to the scene, where I found a guy bending over someone in his driveway. He had both hands applying pressure to the victim's chest. I ran forward with some other officers who had arrived at the same time I did and looked down.

It was Adrian.

Blood pooled on the ground beneath him, soaking his gray shirt and black pants. I took over holding pressure on his chest, still trying to wrap my head around the fact that someone had just tried to murder him. Pressing as hard as I could was all I could do to keep Adrian—a young Hispanic kid who was turning as pale as the concrete below him—alive.

Adrian started to foam at the mouth. He was dying. I looked into his eyes and saw all the fear there, but he couldn't talk at all. It seemed like an eternity before the ambulance arrived. I had to slap Adrian's face multiple times.

"Stay with me," I said to this kid who was like my little brother. "Stay with me."

Adrian was rushed to the hospital where he was immediately taken back to the operating room. I followed him there with a heavy heart and waited impatiently for news, praying for the miracle Adrian would need to survive. Lost in my own thoughts, I didn't notice an elderly woman approaching me.

"Are you Officer Tillman?" she asked.

"Yes, I am," I answered, looking up. "How did you know?"

"Adrian talks about you all the time," she said. It was Adrian's grandmother.

The weight on my heart grew heavier. I'd made more of an impact on Adrian's life than I had realized. By the time I left the hospital that

INTRODUCTION

night, I learned that he'd lost two quarts of blood. His survival was still uncertain, and the odds weren't in his favor.

Confession. There were days when I wondered whether or not this work was worth it. The stress, sleepless nights, and the way this world could be so cruel at times made me question whether or not I had chosen the right profession. After all, trying to be all things to all people can take a toll on even the most dedicated police officers. If you have ever been at a similar crossroads in life then maybe you can relate.

That is where I found myself.

Out of all the possible places on earth, I met my wife (Honey) in Las Vegas. We started dating, and I caught her looking at me a lot (actually it was the other way around). But she always seemed to be seeing something else – something that was me, but more.

Before long, she started calling me "Happy Eyes." I finally asked her what it meant.

"It always seems like you're happy," she said. "You don't even have to have a smile on your face, but your eyes say everything. Like you see the world the way it could be."

Kimberly is my everything, and I wouldn't have had any success without her. So it's no surprise that her words stuck with me. She has seen the best in me from day one; she's my constant assurance that no matter what gets thrown at me, life is good. And yes—her insight brought me to a realization.

I can look at the world and see a glass that's half-full or I can see it as half-empty. That is a choice I got to make every single day.

If I was going to become all things to all people, then I was going to choose to see the best in them, even when it felt like an impossible task. It didn't have to mean

> When we choose to uncover someone else's best, it can transcend into them seeing our best

becoming their friend. It meant I was going to have to use my Happy Eyes. The same eyes that Kimberly saw in me.

Choosing to see the best in a person takes some extra digging but uncovering that "best" allows us to lead with love, empathy, and respect in ways we never have before. Moreover, when we choose to uncover someone else's best, it can transcend into them seeing our best, just like Adrian and Adrian's grandmother saw the best in me.

My hope is that this book will inspire you to use your eyes to see the best in others and to choose to be all things to all people.

CHAPTER 1

A Bridge Between Us

Your Mission, Should You Choose to Accept It

I'm going to tell you what happened to Adrian. But first I want you to do a quick experiment: take a minute to scroll through your social media feeds.

Yes, I know you've just picked up this book. You've just opened the front cover, bypassed the copyright page, the title page, and perhaps even read the dedication. You've pried yourself from your phone and settled in to *read*, darn it, and here I am, encouraging you to put this book down and re-enter the vortex.

Well, not quite. I'm actually giving you a mission. You're being tasked with uncovering some truth about yourself. How many accounts do you follow? Why do you follow them?

Don't worry—there are no right or wrong answers here. But if you're like most of us, you follow people who have one thing in common: *they're like you.*

They're like you, or they express beliefs that you share, or they post content that you like: quotes to ponder, the latest news in sports, funny memes. Whatever it is, some part of you connects with their content in some way. And doesn't it feel good when that happens?

The algorithms controlling what we see in our feeds certainly must think so (in whatever way an algorithm "thinks" at all). With your every like, follow, and repost, the algorithms learn more about what kind of content or accounts you're likely to engage with. They get a pretty solid grasp on what you want to see—and that's what they show you. Before long, most of the content that doesn't jive with who you are and what you believe gets filtered out of what you see as the algorithms funnel content your way.

Which, honestly, can be really fun and exciting. Stumbling upon our new favorite artist, or up-and-coming musician, or podcast can be a delight. If we've been looking for ways to perfect our golf swing, the experience can even be educational.

So: what's wrong with this picture?

The short answer may surprise you: *There is nothing wrong with seeking out people like you.* Surrounding ourselves with people who are like us is the most natural, human thing in the world.

In fact, we crave community with others who dress, talk, think, and look like us. Whether we realize it consciously, we long for connection with those who participate in the same traditions, religions, and activities as we do, and for good reasons. Back when we were all hunter-gatherers, shared interests banded us together and helped us survive. These days, we find comfort, validation, and enjoyment through what we have in common. And in a world full of pandemic-induced isolation, division, and socio-political opposition, we *need* those bridges to one another. Badly.

But here's the flip side: if we only build them between ourselves and people who are like us, we're robbing ourselves of opportunity. Reaching out and forming connections with others like you on social media, in your schools, communities, and churches *is a wonderful thing.* Keep doing that. Never, *ever* let anyone stop you from loving and connecting with your people.

Just...don't stop there. Don't let the fulfillment you find in those relationships convince you they're the only ones that matter.

Beyond the Funnel

Recently I was listening to a podcast. The host was interviewing two Black men, and before long what had begun as a right-versus-left debate about police quickly became a conversation about Black-on-Black crime. The exchange unfolded like so many others have before.

"Police aren't that bad."

"Police *are* that bad."

"Well, what about Black-on-Black crime? Why isn't the left dealing with that?"

"Why isn't the right concerned that we're being killed at an unprecedented rate?"

This is the pattern, right? Anyone aware of the conversations around race and police brutality in this country will recognize it immediately, just like I did. Predictably, the guy on the right brought it to Chicago—another common touchpoint in conversations about Black-on-Black crime (and crime rates in general). I considered moving on to a different episode.

Then, out of the blue, things got interesting.

"Have you ever been to Chicago?" the host asked the guy on the right. "Have you seen any of the programs that are going on there to address violence in the community?"

Unsurprisingly, the guy dodged the question by steamrolling ahead with a bunch of statistics about crime, and the conversation moved forward exactly like most do.

But my attention snagged on the host's question and wouldn't let go.

For me, that tiny blip in the narrative confirmed something. The conversation wasn't *really* about "right" or "left" at all. It wasn't even truly about police behavior, or Black-on-Black crime, or any of the other buzzwords that were being bandied about. It was about *opportunity*.

By posing that question, the host had actually offered something of rare and exceeding value: the chance to *look* at the "problem" of right/left, minority/majority discussions from a different perspective. In other words, he was asking his guest to see past the funnel of sameness he'd built for himself.

Look—I don't want to put words in that guest's mouth, but it seems likely to me that he *didn't actually know* any of those programs existed. He seemed too cocooned by his own beliefs to be aware that there were, in fact, initiatives in Chicago, and that they target the exact problem he was using as a platform.

And here's the thing: *if you don't know whether these programs exist, how can you say they don't?*

An Invitation

The host's question clicked with me for another reason. In essence, he made the same argument that I make whenever someone says to me, "I've never seen a good police officer," or "You never see any police officers calling out other officers' bad behavior."

"Are you looking for those officers?" I ask. "Do you seek them out on social media or in your communities?"

Many times, my questions are met with the same bob-and-weave maneuvering that I heard on that podcast: a litany of statistics, an argument too deeply entrenched in its well-worn groove to be jolted out into new territory. Because people do what we humans naturally do—surround ourselves with people who share our beliefs and values—and we often miss the opportunity to "visit" our own metaphorical Chicago and see it for ourselves.

But here's the thing. If we don't go there—if we don't know what people are doing and saying outside our funnel, if we don't talk to them, associate with them, or hear what they have to say—how can we expect to see it? If we continue living in a "reality" of our own creation, how do we know other realities even exist?

These are extremely uncomfortable questions, right? I mean, they just *are*. We live in a society of polarized opinions. The atmosphere all around us seems determined to reinforce division and widen the gap between one side and the other, which can make bridge-building seem like an impossible task. In fact, most of what's in the mainstream makes us think we must pick a side—be it left or right—and hold our ground, forcefully and with deaf ears. We're expected to claim our side of the Grand Canyon and throw bombs across the divide.

I invite you to consider another opportunity.

The Impossible is Possible

I believe we're not as far left and as far right as the mainstream would have us think. Maybe we're all a little off to the right or left, but aren't most of us actually standing on that middle ground? If I'm right, the distance from me to you isn't that far. Reaching across the aisle, building that bridge, is possible.

It just takes love, empathy, and respect.

This book is never going to try and convince or force you to change your beliefs. That's just not what I'm about. It also isn't attempting to gloss over facts, ignore that they exist, or distort them to advance an agenda. We can't brush over facts, but we must be able to separate them from emotion.

What I hope you'll come to realize is that you can look and hear and even actively listen to other people's opinions, beliefs, and feelings without letting go of your own. Hearing someone out and trying to understand where they're coming from doesn't require that you conform. All it asks is that you see someone first as a *person*, and not a belief system. Focusing on them as a human will allow you to develop a relationship—a bridge—without either of you having to change.

I've experienced this truth a hundred different ways over my time as a police officer. None so viscerally, perhaps, as when Adrian was shot.

Early the next day, I called the hospital to check on him. Every ring of the phone felt like an eternity, and I prepared myself to hear the worst: *Adrian didn't make it through the night.* I heard a soft *click* as someone picked up the line.

> Hearing someone out and trying to understand where they're coming from doesn't require that you conform. All it asks is that you see someone first as a *person*, and not a belief system.

"Officer Tillman," a voice said, "that was crazy, right?"

It was Adrian. He'd survived. I went straight to the mall and bought Adrian a hat, and then I drove to the hospital to see him for myself. While I was there, Adrian's dad came into the room to check on his son's well-being. Our cat-and-mouse history hadn't changed, but that day, sitting shoulder-to-shoulder beside Adrian's hospital bed amid beeping monitors and the bustle of healthcare workers, I wasn't concerned with any of it.

I wasn't looking at Adrian's dad as a former (or potentially future) offender.

I wasn't sitting beside a "criminal."

I was supporting a father who loved his son.

That love was a bridge between us. It didn't rewrite our history or the possibility that we might find ourselves at odds in the future. But it did allow us to celebrate the blessing of Adrian's survival.

Together.

A Way Forward

Because of my cultural upbringing, because of places I've seen or things I've experienced, I may have a different truth than you do. For the same reasons, Adrian's father's truth is probably different from mine. His opinions were formed out of different experiences. I don't condone his crimes, but that doesn't mean I can't extend the same love, empathy, and respect to him that I would to someone who shares my beliefs and values.

Our beliefs, opinions, and feelings are important, but they don't all have to be the same. Even though I may not agree with you, I can still try to understand why you feel the way you do. When I do, that understanding is a bridge between us—a connection that's built on something even more important than what either of us believes.

My friend, that connection *matters*.

Before our wedding, my beautiful wife Kimberly and I went to premarital counseling. I'll never forget the experience.

"If you want to do this the right way," the counselor said, "the first thing you have to understand is that you're going to have arguments. That's not a 'maybe;' it's a certainty. Issues will arise in your house."

The counselor's words definitely got my attention. But it was what he said next that really made an impact.

"Having differences in opinion doesn't make either of you *wrong*," he continued. "It just makes you different. And the sooner you accept that, the sooner you'll be able to reconcile and move forward."

He was right. There's a difference between *wrong* and *different*.

The sooner we come to terms with that, the sooner we can move forward in reconciliation.

And it all starts with love.

CHAPTER 2

Why Connection Matters

Kayla.

A few years ago, my precinct was getting regular calls about a teenage girl who was constantly strung out on drugs. As a police officer, I come in contact with a lot of people who suffer from substance abuse. This girl, Kayla, was sixteen or seventeen. Each time we responded to a call on her she cussed at us, fought with us, even spit on us.

Every time I saw Kayla, I applied one of my dad's favorite principles. "When you look at others," he'd say, "you've got to see your mom, your dad, your brother, your sister, your cousin. And you have to treat them as if they were your family." Seeing my own family member in Kayla helped me find grace and mercy in our interaction.

One day, we arrested her. She was high; she fought us the whole way into the police car. On the way back to the precinct, I felt a tug in my heart. My instincts reminded me that there are always spiritual things at work in our relationships, nudges that we don't always understand. That day, for me, the nudge showed up as an overwhelming urge to play worship music over the stereo. So I did.

"Stop," Kayla shouted at me, high and combative. "Turn it *off*."

The thing was, I trusted the quiet voice that told me to continue caring for her. I hoped for a spiritual breakthrough in her opposition, so I prayed for her and continued driving.

And I left the music on.

It would be years before I learned just how that moment would change both our lives.

What it Takes to Win Someone Over

What does it take to win someone over? The short answer is that it takes authentically connecting with them.

On some level we all know this, right? Maybe we know it consciously—we've read books, attended training or classes, and actively tried to become better at it. Or maybe we only know it instinctively, by a feeling that hits us in the gut when a connection rings true.

But there's a lot more that goes into it.

Whether you're actively attempting to create an authentic connection, or it just organically happens, connecting requires something from you. For instance, you have to be vulnerable. You can't keep your guard up and your emotions in check and hope to connect with someone. It just won't happen that way.

Connection also takes a willingness to see beyond beliefs and topics. We often get so hung up on another person's viewpoints, values, and lifestyle that we miss out on the actual *human* that that person is. Our beliefs and value systems are established early on, during childhood. They're determined by our upbringing, the neighborhoods in which we grew up, the TV or movies we watched together with our friends and families—all kinds of things. By the time we meet each other for the first time as adults, we're only seeing part of the picture. I see that you believe *this* way, and you see that I believe in *that* thing, but unless we dig deeper we won't actually see what matters. We'll see *what* each other believes, but we won't see *why*.

At the end of the day, winning someone over means giving each other the benefit of the doubt.

> At the end of the day, winning someone over means giving each other the benefit of the doubt.

It's another one of those things that's simple in principle but difficult in practice. What I've realized is that you may be completely different from me, and I know in my bones that we will not see eye-to-eye on a lot of different topics. But in many ways, that's irrelevant to the way we relate and connect. Regardless of who you are or what you believe, I can give you the benefit of the doubt. If I choose to, I can find a way to relate to you, human to human. Just like I did with Adrian's dad, I can find some common ground.

When we get caught up in seeing someone as a certain belief or set of values, we miss the opportunity to connect. But a person is *not* a belief—they're a person, with thoughts and feelings, likes and dislikes, hobbies and homes and families. Think of that first, and you *will* find a place to connect, whether it's in lifestyle, shoes, golfing, family—it could be anything.

Scary, But Worth It

But let's be honest. It takes a certain kind of energy to look beyond the big distractions: *this person doesn't look like me, this person doesn't sound like me, this person doesn't think like me*. If we let them, those differences will inspire resistance. We'll be far less likely to invest the energy it takes to try and find similarities with that person.

Why is that, though? It could be because of a lot of things, but I think the biggest reason is *fear*. I think most of us feel as though the moment we start associating with someone who's not like us, we start feeling afraid of *disassociating* with the people who are like us.

I experienced that fear the moment I became a police officer. As a Black man, I feared that my community would think I'd sold out and reject me. As a police officer, I was afraid that being friends with men labeled "criminals" by most cops would cause other officers to mistrust my motives and push me out. And, in reality, either of those things could have happened.

So why is connection worth it?

Two reasons. First, it will make you, personally, a more well-rounded individual. Second, it will open up opportunities. Let's separate those two things.

A Well-Rounded Perspective

Becoming more well-rounded helps us navigate life's twists and turns. For example, I'm the son of two Black parents. I grew up in a very specific way, in a very specific culture. My wife is Filipino and Hispanic; she also grew up in a specific culture, but hers was different from mine. At the beginning of our relationship, bringing the two cultures together was a bit difficult because they didn't necessarily jive that well.

But I've had the good fortune of getting to know many people from all sorts of different cultures and walks of life. Forming relationships with each of them broadened my perspective; now I've seen people experiencing things I never did when I grew up. That helps me be a more successful husband, father, and friend.

The Simple Math of Opportunity

The broader our perspective, the more open we are to expanding our circle of relationships. Here's the simple math: connecting with more and more people brings more and more opportunities. I've connected with people who have been convicted of crimes and had the privilege of walking in friendship with them. I've also established great relationships with people who orbit entirely different spheres of life, like NFL legends Dak Prescott and Michael Strahan. I've even been interviewed by Oprah. And all those connections, in one way or another, led me to write this book for you.

In other words, there's so much value in connecting with others.

Remember Kayla? Fast forward five years from her arrest to the day a woman in her early twenties entered my police department. "Do you know where Officer Tillman is?" she asked a new officer in the station.

"He's only working part time right now," the other officer answered, "and he isn't here today."

"Could you send him a message for me?" She took out her phone and began recording a video. "Hey, Officer Tillman. This is Kayla. I just wanted you to know that day you played worship music and prayed for me changed my life. I'm five years sober now. I went on to establish my own group home for women who struggle with substance abuse. You cared when no one else did, and it changed my life forever."

The world tells us that some relationships don't matter. I'm here to tell you that the way we handle every relationship has a ripple effect. We don't always see it, but the difference we make in someone's life can be positive or negative. My interaction with Kayla changed her life and mine—and also opened up opportunities for so many others. If I'd stayed in my comfort zone, I would never have learned just how powerful connections can be.

One Percent

That's not to say every single connection you make will have the same kind of impact. One morning during my teen years, my dad gave me a ride to high school. That day, he asked me to think about my friends.

"Unfortunately," he said, "the friends you have today may not be your friends tomorrow. They could be locked up tomorrow. They could be dead tomorrow or strung out on drugs. But your friends today could *also* be successful business owners tomorrow. They might go on and change the world in ways we never expected. Not everyone will want to do the right things, but I want you to recognize that you have the ability to make an impact in every single one of their lives. And that impact you make? It could change your life, too."

I apply that philosophy to my life every day. I think about it in terms of connecting with the 1 percent of people who change 99 percent of the world. In our daily lives, we can't know who will turn out to be the next Steve Jobs or Martin Luther King Jr. We should remember that in our connections with others—especially when investing energy to make a connection in the first place feels difficult, misplaced, or even wasted. Regardless of how you feel personally, your investment can reap a return beyond your wildest imaginings.

But that will only happen if you *make the investment in the first place.*

All Things to All People

As humans, we don't always want to invest the energy. We're tired, we're irritated, we're full of doubt that we'll be able to make a difference. But scripture tells us to *become all things to all people,* so that we might win them over and share the blessings of Christ. The apostle Paul became like a Jew to win the Jews. He became like one under the law to win those who were under the law. He became weak to win the weak. All for the sake of the gospel.

We tend to see this world through a distorted lens—one that convinces us we should only keep company with others who are like minded, who see and hear and speak like us. Christians make this mistake all the time. Finding community with other Christians is wonderful and necessary—in fact, we're called to it. But at the same time, we must go out and find the lost.

Paul was always *Paul*, but he followed Jesus' example and leveled with everyone he met. After all, Jesus was still Jesus when He broke bread with tax collectors, and it didn't keep Him from being with them in their homes. Jesus was still Jesus when He sat with the woman at the well; no amount of dirt would have kept Him away.

In every situation, He was exactly the Jesus He needed to be to show love and compassion and to pour into the lives of the people who needed Him most.

And that's what we need to do, too.

The Price of Contention

Real talk: trying to see from everyone's perspective will cost you. Becoming all things to all people will cost you. Stepping out of your comfort zone to love and empathize with others *will cost you*.

Simply put, you will lose people.

The bright side is that you'll gain more than you lose. But the reality is that those losses will still hurt. So you have to dig deep. You have to ask yourself whether the loss of some is worth the greater gain.

As a Black police officer, I have experienced loss on all sides. From a cultural perspective, I'm a sellout to "the man." Every time I talk about good, justified police work, I'm a pig, an Uncle Tom, a coon. On the other hand, when I call out bad police work and admit when we've messed up, I am a new age, "woke" officer to some of my partners in law enforcement. I'm still a sellout, but this time to liberal ideologies and far-left agendas. To these officers, I'm nothing more than a "bootlicker."

I've also lost friends. Once again, the fear of loss looms large. If you're going out there and doing something no one else wants to do—being the bridge, reaching across lines—it's likely you'll experience it.

When I became a police officer, I fell out with one of my very best friends. We stopped talking and had no contact for years.

Believe me, I felt that loss. It was incredibly painful. But it also presented me with a choice: conform to their beliefs and make things pleasing for them to hear, or keep my eyes on the big picture in order to win more people in the long run. I opted for the latter. And, eventually, one of the people I won was a friend I'd lost.

It's the same with interracial couples. There is fear in bringing home someone of a different race. Will your family and community reject them? Will they now reject you, too? Maybe your family will look at you differently. Maybe your neighborhood will look at your family differently (there's that ripple effect again). Regardless, you're paying a price.

But if you break through those barriers, the greater good compensates for the cost. In my case, the love between my wife and me has expanded my family's cultural paradigm and opened up new ways for us to appreciate each other and enjoy life together.

When we intentionally connect with others, blessings abound.

Rewards of Connection (Spiritual)

When we reach beyond what feels comfortable and normal for us to love others—even when it's hard, even in their deficiencies—I believe we are setting ourselves up for rewards in heaven. The Bible talks about these spiritual rewards: the ones we won't see today (perhaps not at all during our time on this earth), but are real nonetheless.

Rewards of Connection (Personal)

Some individuals carry themselves with hesitation. Whether they realize it or not, they enter new situations with uncertainty because they aren't equipped to deal with uncomfortable circumstances and don't know how to respond when those negative feelings arise.

But when you regularly experience the kind of connection I'm describing, you might begin to notice that you walk into a room differently, with a new confidence and a bigger energy. It comes from knowing we can walk into a room of Fortune 500 CEOs *or* a prison and be able to hold ourselves the same way.

I know this because I've done both.

Awhile back, I had the opportunity to speak at a prison, to about 240 incarcerated individuals. While there, I had one-on-one conversations with a fifty-six-year-old prominent leader in the Mexican mafia who'd been jailed since he was sixteen years old and a twenty-four-year-old who had been sentenced to 140 years to life. It was admittedly an uncomfortable situation, but I was able to walk into that fortified place and remain comfortable in my own skin. I was confident in who I was and in the knowledge that I didn't have to change myself or conform my beliefs to fit in.

On the other hand, I've always felt belonging in my friendships with Dak Prescott and Michael Strahan. I felt confident and worthy during that interview with Oprah, who is arguably one of the most prominent public figures the world has ever known. Oprah wasn't the only celebrity on the call either. Tyler Perry and other notable figures were there, too, and in our conversations, I was able to feel confident and like I belonged.

And when you do that, people will notice.

Michael and I worked on a project together for a while before we ever met in person. The first time we met face-to-face, he invited me to go golfing with him and some of his friends. The group included a couple of high-powered executives, one from 21st Century Fox. As intimidating as that set-up could sound—all these guys orbiting the stratosphere of celebrity and power, and me, a regular police officer from California—we had a great time.

"Man," Michael said after the match had ended. "You can really hold your own."

When you are yourself and don't strive to live up to someone else's expectations for you, "holding your own" becomes natural.

Rewards of Connection (Tangible)

Developing relationships with others outside my comfort zone has also given me tangible rewards by helping me establish my business and providing success for my family and others. I consult with Matthew McConaughey's *Just Keep Living Foundation* and Dak's Faith Foundation, among others.

Heart Check

But here's the thing: you can't go into relationships looking to gain rewards. In other words, rewards are the *byproduct* of connection. If your heart is purely looking to gain something from connecting with someone else, that someone will smell it on you a mile away. They'll likely put you in the same category as all the other inauthentic people in their lives.

> Rewards are the *byproduct* of connection.

And no matter how hard you try to connect, they'll resist.

Look—even when you're practicing *authentic* connection, resistance can come in the places you least expect.

Adele.

In my seventh or eighth year of speaking, I was giving a presentation at a middle school. Middle schoolers can be a rowdy bunch, but by that time in my career, I felt like I'd mastered the art of holding their attention (like I tell everyone—if you can speak to police officers, you can speak to anyone). True to form, these kids were loving it. I could see from the expressions on their faces that my presentation was rolling off without a hitch, because they were having a *blast*.

Then, towards the end, a young African American girl raised her hand.

"I have a question."

"OK," I said. "It isn't question time yet, but go ahead."

This girl—we'll call her Adele—was ready to rumble. She began asking questions about which lives matter when they're unjustifiably killed by police, and then she started naming names. *Oh, crap*, I thought. *We're in completely different territory now.*

"I want to commend you for standing up for something you believe in so passionately," I began, doing my best to diffuse the situation, "and for bringing it up in front of your friends. That takes a lot of courage."

My words did not fall on fertile ground. I could see it on her face: *No.* She turned to all the other kids, and the principal started sweating bullets.

"How can you all sit here and laugh and have a great time when we're talking about police brutality?" she demanded.

Her questions landed hard; I continued to answer as best I could, and before long Adele and I were locked in a verbal tennis match. The entire school watched as we went back and forth, back and forth.

"I love your questions," I finally said. "I'm not trying to make light of police brutality—I'm trying to educate everyone. How about you let me finish my presentation, and you and I can talk after."

At that, I got a round of applause from the rest of the auditorium. By respectfully battling it out with this thirteen-year-old girl, I'd won their empathy.

Afterwards, I did speak with Adele. She'd come to my presentation prepared, and her entire argument was written out on the paper she carried. Although I did my best to answer her questions, she stuck to her point.

After a while I understood that she wasn't actually listening to me. She had her own agenda. No matter what I said, she wasn't going to listen to me. I thanked her again, told her I appreciated her, and we ended our conversation.

I might have been the one focused on educating that day, but I learned an important lesson. Sometimes, despite our authenticity and desire to connect, we will be unsuccessful. We'll have to know when to walk away. With Adele, every inch of me wanted to say *exactly* what Ryan Tillman thought. If I'd done that, I would have caused irreparable damage.

Salvaging those moments requires that we listen, discern a person's heart and intentions, and discover that the battle we're fighting is not ready to be won *right now*. If we can do that, it might be possible to come back and connect at a different time, under different circumstances.

This is another way of acknowledging the strategic thinking that happens when we're making connections. I had to step back from my own emotions and assess the situation with Adele. I had to understand that wherever she was coming from made her determined to fight a certain battle that day. I had—and still have—empathy for that. It guided my strategy to do the most possible good in that moment—the only thing that could affect her in a positive way—and end the conversation.

Meeting Others at Pivotal Moments

I met Adele at a pivotal moment in her life. These moments are different for everyone. Depending on your perspective, they can look like the biggest deal in the world, or they can seem entirely insignificant.

We meet people—or they meet us—in pivotal moments every day. Each one is a crossroads: it can go really right or really wrong. So much of that is up to us. Our real-time reactions can make all the difference in the world to someone else. The key to making things go right for another person is to step away from *our* experience of *their* moment. That way, we can be empathetic to the way they're living it.

And the thing is, when you take a second in the situation to process what's best for that person, you never know what you might be doing for them.

Or what they might do for you.

CHAPTER 3

It Starts With Love

Gary.
As pivotal moments go, a child abuse investigation in your family is one of the biggest. Personally, responding to a child abuse situation at work puts me on edge. Any time I see someone take advantage of another person, I absolutely hate it. It makes me incredibly angry—especially when it happens to a kid. Child abuse falls into my no-fly zone.

And yet there I was, assisting my partner one day on a child abuse call.

Chelsea, a sixteen-year-old girl, had called the police on her father, Gary. When we arrived at the scene, she had a small bloody nose but otherwise appeared unharmed. My partner, who was taking the lead on this particular investigation, took Chelsea's statement while I stood with Gary and made sure the situation didn't escalate.

Initially, I didn't start much conversation—although Gary was an African American gentleman and we could've connected over that, my focus was on making sure my partner was safe while she conducted her investigation rather than getting to know the man accused of abuse. But as I began to look around, I noticed that the house was very clean and well-kept. I saw that his entertainment system was loaded with books—several of which were written by Tony Evans, a Texas pastor I've always admired.

And there it was. Despite my reluctance, connection found me that day.

"I see you like Tony Evans," I said. "I love that guy. He's such a good, godly man."

Gary looked up. "I listen to him every day on my way to work."

We eased into a dialogue about Pastor Evans and even discovered our mutual esteem for a particular book, *Kingdom Man*. One by one, the barriers between Gary and me began to fall until I was no longer talking to a *criminal* or a *child abuser*. I was talking with a father of five.

Meanwhile, Gary's kids were lobbing accusations at each other.

One blamed everything on Chelsea and said she shouldn't have called the police—that she should *never* call the police. From the other side of the room, another sister reminded everyone that their dad was the one who hit Chelsea, so she *should* have called. Chelsea's mom was in the middle, torn between her kids and stuck in the worst day of her life.

I started asking Gary about what happened.

"Chelsea's been sneaking guys into the house," he admitted, "and just the other day she called my wife the B-word and a whore. We're trying to help her grow into a young lady, but she continues to disrespect her own body. And today I just…lost it. I slapped her in the face because *I lost it*."

In the back of my mind, I could see the situation from Gary's perspective. When I stepped into the shoes of a father trying to raise a daughter, I could see how his reaction was understandable, even if it was still wrong. As an officer of the law, I couldn't take his side of the story as unadulterated truth, but I felt compassion for this person who strove to do the right thing but lost control in a fraught situation.

Gary *was* telling the truth. After speaking with Chelsea, my partner corroborated his story. Still, this was a situation involving child abuse.

That meant Gary's culpability would be decided by the courts. I knew I had no choice about what happened next for Gary, but I also knew I could still show him and his family love.

"I completely understand why you lost your cool today," I said, pulling Gary aside. "I understand the human side of what you did. Unfortunately, though, we're still going to have to arrest you."

He nodded.

"But your whole family is here," I continued. "I don't want them, or your neighbors, or anyone else to watch you get hauled out in handcuffs and see you as a criminal, because that's not what you are. You're a hard-working father who's trying to provide for them and doing his best. So we're going to do it a different way. We're going to be safe. We're going to walk to my partner's car, and I'm not going to put handcuffs on you until we get there so no one has to see you in them. And now I need to know: can I trust you enough to do that?"

"Yes," he said. "I really appreciate that, Officer Tillman."

Gary, my partner, and I walked to the car exactly as planned. Right before I put the handcuffs on him, we prayed together. "Things are going to be OK," I said. "I know this is a terrible situation, but everything will work out."

My partner drove away with Gary in the backseat of her cruiser and I walked back to my car. I thought my role in the situation was over. As far as I was concerned, the situation *itself* was over. There was nothing left for me to do.

I couldn't have been more wrong.

Why Love?

Leading with God's love in every situation forces us to ask ourselves a question: can you see past the flaws or evil in a person if you truly love them? To state it differently, we could ask whether our love can surpass and *overcome* those flaws.

That might sound strange, but genuinely loving humans for all they are and all they're created to do actually *requires it*. To love each other fully and wholly, we have to get past the flaws that make each of us who we are.

Which—to be fair—is a *huge* deal.

When we've never thought about loving others this way, it helps to make it personal. It's like my dad always said: love the person in front of you like your brother, your mother, your sister, your cousin. Personally, I think about my wife and my kids—the people I love most in the whole world.

Thinking about my kids really helps me put things in perspective because my kids do some crazy things sometimes. Take, for example, the time we had two pet snakes in the house. I've never been a snake guy, so getting them in the first place took some love-forward finessing of my heart, right? Well. Regardless of my personal feelings, the snakes lived as comfortably as anyone else in my house in their terrarium in the kids' room with a heat lamp to keep them warm.

Then one day, I noticed smoke filling the upstairs level.

Where is this coming from? I thought. I started walking toward it, checking for fire as I went. When I entered my kids' room, I found the source of the smoke. The kids had put the heat lamp on the floor—while it was switched *on*—and it had already burned through the carpet and down to the wood subflooring. I immediately switched it off, but internally I was freaking out.

You guys could have burned the house down, I thought.

Truth be told, I was angry. They could've burned the house down! But I also understood that they're *kids*. They hadn't intentionally *tried* to burn down the house—they simply didn't know what they didn't know.

And I love them, and love changes everything when we let it.

That day, my love for my kids slowed me down. It created a space for me to think about what was about to come out of my mouth and how the moment could be better for them. Ultimately, it changed the way I responded. Sure, they got in trouble. Sure, I raised my voice a little. But instead of coming at the situation from a place of anger, I approached the conversation as a way to educate them out of their ignorance.

None of us know everything. We all have blind spots and are ignorant about something (or many things). Knowing this and responding with love allows us to do what I did that day. We can slow ourselves down, try to process what a person is saying, and cover whatever ignorance they have.

When I say "cover," I mean it in a very Biblical sense. In the New Testament, Peter tells us that "love covers a multitude of sins." This is a reference to the way Jesus' love covers us—and that makes it a perfect strategy to think of how we can practice that love in every relationship or connection we have.

Which is exactly what we have to do when we find ourselves in someone's pivotal moments. My kids wouldn't have thought of it this way, but they were in one. When a parent loses their cool, it can cause all kinds of negative fallout.

It's the same in police work. From a tactical perspective, most mistakes—including uses of force—are made when we're moving too fast. So: we're constantly reminded to *slow down, slow down, slow down*.

That can be an admittedly difficult thing to do as a police officer in high-risk, high-emotion situations. But if you're a fellow officer and you're reading this, please hear me when I say *love will slow you down*. On the other side of fast and furious, you're in control of your reaction. And from that calmer place, your wisdom and skill are in the driver's seat.

I'm not saying you need to love everyone you meet in the same way you love your spouse. I'm talking about God's love, which is a *genuine* love for people as humans. Loving someone the way God loves us actually makes it simple to see past their flaws and get to another level with them.

Making Pivotal Moments Go Right

That's also how we can meet someone in their pivotal moment and help things go right instead of wrong: we get on another level with them. Specifically, we get on *their* level. I'm not talking about lowering ourselves—no one is on a pedestal here. I mean we must teach ourselves how to understand where a person is coming from.

This is different from saying you have to be able to relate—because truthfully? You don't, and it's not always a good idea to try (I'll get to that a little later). Relating can only happen if you've been through the same situation, or one so similar that you can identify, on a very real level, with the physical, emotional, or psychological experience someone is having.

Understanding is different. It says, "Hey, I've never been through what you're going through, but I can understand the same emotions you're having because we all share the same emotions, even if we experience them in different circumstances and in different ways."

In other words, understanding is making the effort to learn what another person is trying to process by listening to them. From there, sometimes you can help with a solution. Sometimes listening *is* the solution. But trying to *force* a solution (which can be especially tempting for police officers) can make a pivotal moment go wrong.

Automatically trying to relate to someone in crisis can also break a pivotal moment. Sometimes, people don't want that—they simply want to be able to go through whatever it is they're going through without someone talking over them.

I've learned this in lots of little ways throughout my life, but it really hit home a couple of years ago when my dad and my father-in-law died six months apart from each other.

The circumstances each of them experienced were completely different. My dad's death was slow; he had been diagnosed with multiple sclerosis in 2008. Shortly after, the strongest man I've ever known went from walking, to walking with an unsteady gait, to walking with a cane, to using a walker, to a wheelchair, to a bed, where he ultimately died. It was the hardest thing I've ever had to witness. Then, my father-in-law, who—despite being stern and tough on me when we first met—had become my golfing buddy, close friend, and spiritual mentor, passed two weeks after contracting pneumonia. It was the saddest thing I've ever experienced.

Before losing her father, my wife had never really experienced that kind of trauma in her life, and it hit her with all the force you can probably imagine. Initially, I thought I knew how to be there for her. My dad had died almost six months to the day of her losing her dad. Plus, I had been going through the trauma of losing him for fourteen years—I had learned a lot about loss and grief, and so I tried to give my wife all the answers and solutions in my arsenal.

But that wasn't what she needed.

I had nearly a decade and a half to come to terms with the fact that my dad would eventually die; when it happened, I was prepared. My wife never had that chance. Although we'd both lost our fathers, our experiences were completely different—and there I was, telling her I could relate to what she was going through. Little wonder my insistence caused some hurt feelings and misunderstandings for both of us.

Eventually, though, I realized that what she needed was a moment to simply *grieve*. She needed to vent. She needed a moment in which someone would just listen without trying to fix what was happening to her.

When I realized that, I stopped trying to relate to her experience of grief and focused instead on the fact that we were both grieving. And that understanding built a new bridge between us.

Leading With Love

When I encourage people to lead with love as a foundation for powerful connection, sometimes they push back. People want to know how they can love someone who they don't know. They think it's impossible to love everyone.

There's a difference between loving someone and liking them, but I believe if you really care about humans, you can love them. So in the face of that argument, I will usually explain things the way my dad did: look at the person as a real brother or sister. Despite the color of their skin or the church they attend, look at them as somebody you genuinely care about.

And I will admit that is not always enough.

Sometimes, love also requires action. Specifically, it requires *pursuit*. And that doesn't always look the way we think it will—sometimes, it looks like the opposite. There's a person in my life—we can call him John —who I love, in the way God calls us to love our neighbors, but do not always like. The way I enact that love is by intentionally holding back and not establishing any sort of relationship with him whatsoever.

If that seems counterintuitive to loving someone, allow me to explain. I know that talking with John will almost always go south. Intentionally disengaging from him doesn't mean I don't care; it means I care enough to choose what's best for us both. We don't have a relationship because it won't be fruitful.

There may be someone in your life you consider an enemy (in fact, there likely is). Real talk: you *can* still love that person even though you don't like them. And expressing your love through inaction doesn't stop you from praying for them, showing them kindness, or any number of things that demonstrate what love looks like. And who knows? You might even win them over in the long run.

Unfortunately, leading without love can be just as impactful as leading with it. A lot of families know this firsthand; some of our biggest social problems are a result of the widespread inability to express affection and love for one another. Let's be real—this is something that especially affects men, and when it does, it causes huge amounts of suffering. Not every man grew up the way I did, watching their father comfortably say, "I love you" to his friends. If more of us had my dad's phenomenal example, I think a lot of the brokenness we experience today could be mended.

In law enforcement, leading with love looks like officers doing things that go against the status quo, like spending time in the communities they serve because they want to, not because they have to. They start going out of their way to get to know these communities—even on their days off.

There's an old saying that to truly know a place and its people, you have to live there. That may be true, but I believe you don't have to live in a community to love on it and take ownership in your relationship with it and treat it as your own.

All you have to do is love it.

Authentically.

The Dangers of Inauthenticity

Love with authenticity is easy to pick out. It's taking the time to know a person—to learn about something that makes them who they are. But what about inauthentic "love?" Without naming names, it's safe to say we don't have to go far to find an example.

We could think about it this way: how many times have you heard a politician promise to do something because they *truly* care about you? As I write this, it's election season. We're seeing politicians everywhere, all the time. They want to be involved in every aspect of your life—until the election is over.

When that happens, have they fulfilled the promises or, at the very least, still seem to be interested in your needs? Maybe. I do believe some politicians have the hearts of the people in mind. But if you're thinking of one who doesn't, and who's only playing the game to get elected, you've witnessed what it's like when someone is inauthentic with others.

In many ways, we've all been guilty of this. That's one reason why it's far better not to over-promise in your zeal to connect. Just be sincere with the person instead. Because when we're trying to form bonds with others, trust—the thing that lets people know you have their best interest at heart—is an absolute requirement. It's the active ingredient in the love, empathy, and respect needed to become all things to all people.

Trust is a beautiful thing, but can only be earned through faithfulness, through small acts of service and kindness, through keeping your promises and showing up when you say you will. It's a foundation to build on, a bridge between us and someone else. That's one reason why love without authenticity is so dangerous—it's one of the best ways to lose a person's trust. And once trust is gone, it may be difficult, or even impossible, to regain it.

You may have relationships in your life in which it seems as though trust has been irreparably broken. If so, there's grace for that. It's impossible to seek and gain the trust of everyone in our lives. Besides—broken trust doesn't mean you absolutely cannot have a relationship with that person. It just means the relationship might look different.

This is Going to Sound So Strange

The day I was called to assist in Gary's house, I was able to build trust with him and his family because I led with love. Trust was critical in that pivotal moment because I needed them to know I was there with their best interests at heart. Once we connected, and the situation was resolved, I thought that was it. The end of my part in Gary's story.

Yeah. That's not exactly how it happened.

While I sat in my car on their block, deciding between sushi or a burger for lunch, the strongest, Holy Spirit-led feeling came over me: I needed to go back into Gary's house and pray for his family.

Man, I remember thinking, *I know that's so weird. Like, the weirdest thing ever. I don't want to.*

If you know Jesus, you know that when the Holy Spirit presses on us it's impossible to ignore. We might think we can run from it, but no. It's not going to happen. And true to form, I could feel *Go back and pray for them* written indelibly on my heart.

"All right," I said. And I got out of the car, went to the door, and knocked. Gary's wife answered.

"Hey," I said. "This is going to sound so strange, so let me just throw that disclaimer out there. But do you mind if I pray for your family?"

Her jaw dropped. "Oh my goodness. I was praying that you would come back and pray with us."

Wow.

Inside, things were tense. There was a bad energy in the house, and I think everyone sensed it. We all grabbed hands and prayed. Gary's wife started crying; soon all the kids were crying with her.

"Look," I said when we'd finished, "I know your dad's not a bad guy, and I'm so sad you all had to take the brunt of his emotion today. But things will get better."

We hugged, and they thanked me for coming back. "We needed that, Officer Tillman," they said.

Eventually, I left, convinced I was actually done this time.

Turns out, though, the situation wasn't done with me.

CHAPTER 4

Leading With Empathy

Braden.
    I've been a part of my department's crisis negotiation team for about four years. One day while I was on duty, a call came over the radio: a male perpetrator had fled from officers in a vehicle all the way to his home, where he'd barricaded himself and refused to come out. I immediately responded and turned my car toward the unfolding crisis.

My primary focus as a negotiator in these situations is to prevent a tactical response that could result in people getting hurt—and that means I communicate with perpetrators in a very specific way: trying to resonate with the guy who's afraid as opposed to the suspect who committed a crime. That means creating an organic interaction and communicating as human to human instead of officer to suspect.

I get nervous every time. There are a lot of unknowns in these scenarios. One wrong move on my part and I could be the guy who sets the person off and causes them to escalate, kill themselves, or create a situation in which we have to use force. The pressure is always on.

As I drove, I asked the dispatcher questions about who the man was and why he was wanted—anything that might give me clues about his potential future, his possibility for redemption, and how I could best form a meaningful connection. In moments like these, connecting with the Holy Spirit suppresses the side of me that would talk over people to problem solve. Prayer is a way to bring God forward and let Him take the wheel.

"God, give me the words to speak," I prayed. "Allow them to be Your words and not mine. I want Braden to feel the comfort You give."

It was midday when I arrived at the scene, and the entire neighborhood was there, cell phones poised to capture the confrontation. I heard people talking; I felt them watching. We were center stage, and our audience was waiting to see how the "performance" would unfold.

Several of my partners had already spent about twenty or thirty minutes trying to talk to the suspect. They weren't getting anywhere. I made contact with him over the phone and began a dialogue.

"Hey, this is Ryan," I said. "What's going on?"

Braden was a young guy. There was no doubt he'd committed some crimes, and he was afraid of going to jail.

By that point in my life, I had already spent a lot of time working with young people, both as a speaker and in my job as an officer at the high school. From those experiences, I knew the best thing I could do was let Braden do most of the talking.

So I listened and listened, until Braden grew quiet.

"Man," I said finally, "I understand that you're afraid right now. Everyone here knows you're afraid of what's going to happen when the police come."

Braden didn't respond, but I could tell his hard exterior was beginning to soften.

"If you're hearing me," I continued, "understand that I care and that your safety is my number one priority. I'm not going to say it might not be difficult for you. You're going to have to go to jail for a little bit. But that's not the end of the road for you. There are things you can do to get yourself on the right path. If you're truly committed and care enough to fight for that, I know you can do it."

Braden's walls began to crumble, then fall. He said he was willing to come out of the house, where a tactical team was waiting to take him into custody.

"Braden," I said, "when you come out, you have to listen to what the other officers tell you to do. But first, I will meet you at your front door. I'll be right outside waiting for you, waiting to shake your hand like a man."

Sure enough, he listened.

He came out of the house, and I was there waiting to keep my promise.

Empathy is a Requirement, Not a Choice

I believe you picked up this book for a reason. There is something in you that believes in the power of connection; there is something in you that is called to be all things to all people, and you're ready to dive deep into what that takes. All right. I'm with you.

So: empathy.

We all have different experiences as we walk our path through this earth. That's the cause of so much contention sometimes, isn't it? It's like we've said before: different experiences give us different contexts, and we make decisions, speak, and act from them. And a lot of times, that means we disagree about…nearly everything.

Making an authentic, lasting connection with another person requires trust. It's simply non-negotiable—without it, a person will never feel safe enough with you to be *vulnerable* with you. And let me just say this now: if a person can't feel vulnerable with you, you'll never really get to know them. Forming the kind of connection it takes to win them over will be impossible.

A person has to know they can be vulnerable with you. The only way that can happen is empathy: putting yourself in their shoes so you can understand the context they're speaking and acting from.

Empathy is Misunderstood

So many times, we *do* try. We attempt to see the world through another person's eyes and identify with their point of view. The thing is—and I believe this to my core—empathy is almost always misunderstood. We tend to associate empathy with "I've gone through this" or "I've experienced that." But empathy is so much more about the emotions an experience creates and less about the experience itself.

> Empathy is so much more about the emotions an experience creates and less about the experience itself.

In fact, focusing on experience is the biggest way connection can go wrong. Regardless of who we're talking to, there's a solid chance our experiences won't match up with theirs. This is why people lash out sometimes. "You have no clue what I'm going through right now," they say. "Your experience is way different from mine, so stop trying to use that as a way to gain my trust or understand where I'm coming from."

That reaction is a version of what my wife, Kimberly, and I experienced as we processed our fathers' deaths. Although we both lost a father, the circumstances—and therefore our experiences—were completely different. What ultimately resolved the hurt and misunderstanding between us then is the same thing I'm telling you now: to empathize with someone, put yourself in their shoes from an *emotional* standpoint.

Sharing your emotional experiences with someone is how you develop empathy with them. It will build a bridge without setting off their "you don't know what I'm going through" defenses. This is because it's far more authentic. As human beings, we are all created to experience the same emotions. The circumstances that bring them on may be different, but grief, loss, love, anger, fear, excitement, wonder—those are universal.

Meet Emotional Trauma with Emotion

Think about the strife that exists between law enforcement and the communities they serve. Law enforcement typically meets that strife by saying, "We're not bad, we just have a few bad apples that have ruined the batch. The majority of us are good."

As we all know by now, this response doesn't work.

Say that to someone who isn't a fan of police officers, and they won't experience empathy or understanding. All they'll see is someone trying to defend their position. And, on the flip side, if you're the one talking about "bad apples," it's unlikely you'll feel anything but frustration when people don't take you at your word and believe the majority in the profession *are good*.

Here's the thing. If I want to win someone over, I have to learn how to understand *why* their belief system is what it is—why they feel the way they feel—even if it's not *my* belief system. In the case of law enforcement, we often fail to do that. We fail to recognize that in some way, shape, or form—whether indirectly through videos they watch on social media or directly, through a personal experience—the community we serve has experienced an emotional trauma attached to law enforcement, and that trauma caused their negative feelings. It's why they're up in arms (sometimes literally).

The nature of law enforcement is such that many officers have never had the same experiences that caused these feelings. That means trying to reach these communities by saying "I get where you're coming from" is never going to work.

To build bridges and begin healing these wounds, we must meet emotional trauma with emotion.

That's why I often begin my presentations and workshops with an apology. "I'm sorry on behalf of the bad officers," I say. "I'm sorry on behalf of the ones that have caused you the trauma you've experienced. I'm sorry."

Notice that I didn't change my beliefs or compromise who I am to do that. I didn't say, "Police officers are terrible humans," because I don't believe they are. Each time I deliver that apology, I can walk away from the conversation secure in the fact that I'm still the Ryan I was before having it. I simply took a minute to get real with some people in hopes of gaining a better understanding of who they are and why they believe the way they do.

In other words, I put the *person* first.

The result is truly incredible. Just that little bit of humility and dying to self—just that single act of reaching out, emotion to emotion, to say "I'm sorry"—breaks down defenses. Time and again, I have personally felt the tension dissipate. I have witnessed the change on hundreds of faces when skepticism and mistrust are replaced with *wow, he understands me. Maybe I'll listen.*

Hypocrisy vs. Human

Practicing emotion-led empathy allows us to lay down our instincts to judge and take up Christ's commandment to "love our neighbor as ourselves." And that's so, so important, right? Because let's face it: one of the biggest hang-ups people have about Christians is that they're "hypocritical." I've heard this my whole life, and—whether you're a Christian or not—you probably have, too. Maybe you've even felt that way yourself.

The conflict can be extrapolated beyond Christianity, however. As is evident in the strife between law enforcement and their communities, people from one group who attempt to identify with the experiences of others from another group get labeled as hypocrites (or worse).

I believe the tendency to see hypocrisy in others is driven by the fact that one person or group in the equation feels judged. And look—I'm going to be straight with you. *Judgment is not our job.* It won't help you win anyone.

The good news? When we jettison the idea that we can relate to someone else's experience and instead identify with their emotions, it allows them to see you as *not* judgmental.

As a police officer, I routinely make arrests. When that situation arises, I always tell the person I'm not there to judge them. That's not my job. "My job is to perform police work as best I can and to treat you with dignity and respect," I say. More often than not, the empathy I show a person at one of the lowest moments in their life unlocks their vulnerability and trust. They open themselves up.

Imagine the possibilities if all officers met their communities' emotional traumas with emotion. On the flip side, imagine what could happen if communities allowed emotion-led empathy to stop them from seeing officers as bad apples in uniform and start seeing them as *human*.

My YouTube series, *Switched*, is all about putting civilians in the shoes of police officers. We re-enact real scenarios in which they roleplay as the responding officers. Recently, my team re-created a situation that happened in New Mexico. A police officer noticed a pickup with illegally tinted windows and conducted a traffic stop. He approached the passenger side and politely asked the driver to step out of the truck and walk back to the tailgate. The driver complied—he exited the cab and, still on the opposite side of the vehicle from the officer, began walking in pace with him toward the rear.

What the officer didn't know, however, was that the driver was carrying a rifle.

The officer's view was blocked by the truck bed between them, so he couldn't see the driver's hands. Before they reached the tailgate, the driver—now suspect—raised the weapon, executed the officer, and drove away.

It was tragic.

On the *Switched* set, we put several civilians in that officer's role. Every single one of them "got shot." But what was most interesting to me was that afterwards, when we were discussing their experiences, what impacted them the most was not their personal fear or outrage.

"If this was me in real life," one man said, "I'm not coming home to my wife. I'm not coming home to my kids." His words were an acknowledgment: somewhere in New Mexico, there was a *real* wife who is now a widow. There were *real* kids who will never see their dad walk through the front door ever again. It completely changed his perception of law enforcement officers.

For this man and his fellow role-players, it wasn't the *experience* of "getting shot" that changed their hearts and minds—it was the *emotion* of that experience. They became emotionally connected not because they had personally lost someone in a traffic stop, but because they were husbands. Dads. Knowing that another husband and dad had lost his life made everything different.

If empathy and human connection can make that kind of change, what else might it accomplish?

I'm fortunate to have wonderful, beautiful, *real* relationships with people who hold faiths and political beliefs that are polar opposite from mine. And we get along so well because we have a human connection that only empathy can create.

Take it to the Bank

Have you ever walked down the street, caught a scent on the breeze, and landed squarely in a long-forgotten moment? If so, what did it do to your state of mind? Chances are that your emotions followed your nose. Not only were you in the memory, but you also *felt* the memory—both in your senses (maybe not *literally*) and your emotions (likely *very* literally).

Science tells us that our senses are gateways to our decision-making abilities. That's why professional marketers constantly appeal to us at the levels of smell, taste, and touch. But these senses can also help us open a door to connecting with someone, even—or especially—a someone we feel we have nothing in common with or don't even really like.

Obviously, the big one here is to *listen*. If we want to connect, we need to listen. That's a bit of a no-brainer (I hope). But I'm talking about a certain kind of listening: the kind that helps you learn about the person you're speaking with. This listening takes active awareness, being observant, and present.

We all know how easy it can be to get distracted in a conversation (it happens to me, too). The point of this kind of listening is to devote your time and energy to the person talking. Otherwise, you'll miss things. You won't get what you need to formulate an authentic connection.

In the process of listening, I encourage you to utilize *all* your senses. It's almost like going on an expedition, of sorts, or even a treasure hunt: *X marks the spot where I find some way to connect*. Maybe you recognize a person's perfume or cologne—what does that scent mean to you? What memories does it inspire? Maybe you see that they're wearing a certain pair of shoes you like—do you have the same ones? Have you ever seen them in person before?

All these things are tapping into your mental-emotional bank: the place from which you build authentic connections. They also add to that bank, enlarging the balance from which you can make future withdrawals by bringing up things you remember. I encourage you to try it. The person you're talking with will say, "Wow—you remember that?" They'll feel valued because you've just shown them they *are*.

In every context—whether you're a law enforcement officer, a sales professional, a customer service representative, a school official, a family member, or a hopeful new friend—sensory-informed listening will amplify empathy and strengthen connections.

Authentically.

Empathy Has to Care

When empathy is authentic, it cares.

That means trying to understand a person's emotion, even when you can't identify with what they're going through. It means spending less time talking and more time listening carefully, openly, and with your judgment suspended. It also means not being written off as a fraud or a fake by the person you're trying to form a connection with.

The day I responded to Braden's situation, he listened to me—I believe—because the way I listened showed him that I really did care. So many times, our instinct is to rush into offering solutions to a person in crisis. Or we may interrupt the conversation with the thing we've been planning to say all along the second we get a chance. But that's not really listening, is it? Most of the time, it's also not even close to what the person is looking for. When empathy cares, it listens first and without formulating a response ahead of time.

It is also honest. I didn't understand what Braden was going through because I've never run from the police before. I couldn't identify with his exact experience, so I didn't say, "I understand *why* you're afraid." If I had, I would've been lying—the opposite of showing care. Instead, I said "I understand *that* you're afraid."

Ethan.

Late one night I responded to another crisis, this time involving an individual who was suicidal. Ethan had been running in and out of traffic on a busy street with his hands in his pockets. He was possibly armed. I'd been called in by my supervisor, who informed me that another department was already on the scene.

These officers didn't have negotiator training, so they had been barking orders at Ethan to take his hands out of his pockets and get on the ground. They were doing their best, but they simply didn't know how to connect with him. Commands and demands were not going to meet Ethan's actual need (or, for that matter, theirs).

I prayed my usual prayer on the drive over, and an officer I didn't know filled me in when I arrived. "We've been trying to get this guy into custody, but we can't." By that point, Ethan was surrounded by a circle of police cars with their lights and sirens on.

My partner and I began slowing things down. We stopped making demands. I got on a loudspeaker and introduced myself.

Ethan never said a word.

After two and a half hours, he still hadn't spoken at all.

It was one of the most difficult negotiations in my life. The pressure was incredible, of course. Just like with Braden, there was a huge crowd of bystanders and family members with their cell phones out, waiting for things to go wrong. But the worst part was that I didn't know whether my words were resonating. Were my attempts to build a rapport pushing him away? I had no way of knowing.

Then at some point, my secondary negotiator pulled me aside. Ethan's mother had just arrived.

"She told me he's a music producer and he likes jazz," my second said. I started talking to Ethan about jazz. No dice. He still wouldn't budge.

Suddenly, I got a crazy idea. I looked at my watch; it was the middle of the night. I didn't care.

"You know what?" I said. "Why don't we stop talking for a minute and put on some music?"

I instructed the other department to turn off the front lights and the sirens. I didn't want Ethan to become more distracted or afraid than he already was as Miles Davis' *Blue in Green* poured out of the PA system at full volume.

That's when I finally saw it: something was percolating in Ethan's eyes.

Eventually, we picked back up with the negotiation. It was difficult, but in the end, Ethan was taken into custody without being hurt.

Afterward, so many of the people who'd been watching—including his wife—thanked us for showing enough care to try and get to know

Ethan and save his life instead of quickly trying to use force. That one simple act was enough to potentially win not just one person over, but an entire community.

Whether we intend it or not, our actions indirectly teach others a way of moving through the world. It happened that night with Ethan; it happened the day of Braden's arrest. When empathy cares, it's infectious. It can spark the kind of reaction that creates real change.

> When empathy cares, it's infectious. It can spark the kind of reaction that creates real change.

Organic Empathy Comes from Expanding Your Circle

When I was in high school, my track coach, Coach Brock, was one tough guy. He imposed punishing warmups and stared us down like a drill sergeant while we ran them. During stretches, he peppered us with questions and tried to teach us lessons. We all thought he was the bad guy until we realized the method to his madness. He was trying to make us physically *and* mentally strong. Coach Brock genuinely cared about who we were and who we would become.

"Ryan," he'd always say. "You guys got to get off the block."

"I live three miles from here," I'd tell him. "I'm not on the block."

I wasn't being sarcastic; I just didn't know what he meant. It wasn't until college, when I lived in Las Vegas and had the opportunity to play football with people from all walks of life—Alaska, Australia, New York, the Midwest, Ethiopia—that I got Coach's message. He was telling me to expand my cultural circle of friends.

Coach knew how common it is for people to let where they come from or what they look like define the boundaries of who they get to know. He was incredibly savvy about relationship building in that way, and he was right: getting off the block physically and mentally gave me the confidence to build relationships with people who weren't like me.

That's what empathy does. It takes someone who grew up in a really great neighborhood—without a lot of poverty, absent parents, or crime, for example—and helps them form connections with those who grew up differently than they did. Empathy drives them to seek out relationships with people from backgrounds different than theirs.

And what a valuable thing to do, right?

I'm a firm believer that we reap what we sow. Planting seeds in an effort to become more culturally diverse, to know a variety of people, to exist simultaneously as who we are but with love and empathy for everyone around us allows us to learn. To make better connections. Not only do we enrich our own lives, but we also equip ourselves to continue expanding our circles outward.

Organic empathy is powerful in that way.

And, as we'll see in Chapter 5, so is respect.

CHAPTER 5

The Power of Respect

Sam.
I visited Valley State Prison in November of 2022. I'd arrived that day alongside a good friend of mine, Artie. At sixteen, Artie was convicted of killing someone and sentenced to life in prison, where he spent the next twenty-one years. After his release, he completely transformed his life.

Artie invited me that day to speak to the Valley State inmates alongside him and a few friends, who had also spent time in prison. He has a real soft spot for incarcerated individuals. "You commit a crime," he explained, "and the punishment is only punitive. There's no redemption tied to it at all."

I followed Artie and a few of his friends into their world, and that's where I met a kid named Sam. I say "kid," because that's exactly what Sam was. At twenty-two, he was looking to spend the next 140 years of his life incarcerated. However many years of the fourteen-decade sentence he would live to serve, every last one would be spent inside the four walls of that prison.

As we began the event, I kept my eye on Sam. A few minutes into our talk, Artie's friend James asked a question.

"Was the game what you thought it was when you guys were doing what you were doing?" The "game" James referred to was drug dealing. "Was it worth it?" he pressed. "Was being part of a gang and doing all the things you did worth it?"

Every hand in the room shot up—none faster than Sam's—to say, "No. It wasn't worth it."

After the main session, we broke off in small groups. As fate would have it, Sam was in mine. We all settled into a small circle of chairs and I took a breath.

"What brought you all here?" I asked.

For a minute, the group was quiet. Then, finally, Sam spoke up.

"I didn't know how to deal with a lot of the things I was going through," he said. "I joined a gang, and we hurt people so everybody in our neighborhood would give us respect."

Others chimed in. One way or another, the roads that led them to that room all began the same way.

They had all wanted respect.

Respect is Earned, Not Given…Or Is It?

You have to earn *my respect.*

We've all heard that sentence, right? We've heard it from our parents and grandparents. Our teachers. Maybe you've even said it. Maybe you *meant* it.

And who could blame you? I mean, the sentiment is everywhere—movies, music, politics, sports. Setting up respect as a give/take, either/or binary seems like common law. And, as I learned from Sam and the other inmates of Valley State prison, respect is a touchy thing. Get on the wrong side of it, and see how quickly the world around you can spiral out of control and cause dangerous and destructive situations.

As a police officer, I've seen the fallout of that danger firsthand time and again. I have empathy for Sam and the other men I spoke with that day, and I've also been in countless situations in which I'm coming between one person and the others they're trying to harm. And yes—there have been days when police intervention wasn't enough. On those days, I find myself with people who, on the surface, don't seem to deserve my respect at all.

But that's my humanity talking.

Like I've said before, I don't have to agree with someone's actions. I don't have to agree with their beliefs. If you've just committed a heinous crime, I don't have to (and I won't) condone the things you've done. But I can peel back the layers of the situation and intentionally give you my respect before it's been earned.

OK—stay with me. I'm not saying this is easy. I'm not saying I see it all the time, either, especially when we, as officers, are dealing with a person who has taken a life or grievously hurt someone else. It is far easier to think about the people they've hurt and get angry on the victim's behalf. But no amount of disrespect to a perpetrator will undo what they've done.

Perhaps you're holding this book and thinking of someone you could choose to give respect, but don't quite know where to start. I've been there, and I can tell you the process is similar to that of finding empathy, which I described in Chapter 3. Don't try to identify with the experience a person is having. Instead, choose to understand that they are having an emotion, which every human, at one point or another, has had. When we choose to give respect to someone who hasn't earned it, especially if that person has disrespected or even hurt us, we have to see them as someone who is a person *just like us*. We are all people who have made mistakes.

I always think of this in terms of my spiritual life. I am not perfect—I'm a man who has sinned many, many times. And yet God—who *is* perfect and who doesn't need my respect—forgives me over and over again. I fall short all the time, and He meets my failures by *giving me respect*.

When I remember that, how can I *not* do the same for others who have failed me?

Each of us will one day stand before God and be judged. Some of us will also stand before an earthly judge and answer for our crimes. I've said it before, and I'll say it again: judging is not my job. I tell this to every person I drive to jail, and I treat them with common decency. Sometimes, what happens next is astounding.

I find myself getting confessions. I've watched as perpetrators write letters of apology to the victim or their families. Why? Because intentionally giving unearned respect to a person breaks down their walls—and, in these instances, I'm actually helping the victim more than if I'd followed my anger and acted from a place of high emotion (which will never earn anyone's respect). There's a time and place in which to tactically utilize that kind of emotion, but we need to separate when to get stern, stand our ground, and defend ourselves from when to be kind—or even meek.

Be the Lion

When I first became a police officer, others on the force pegged me as too jovial and nice. Officers who had been in the field a long time even warned me to be careful. They didn't know that I grew up in a culturally diverse town, where I had to fight a lot of battles. I had been in a few fistfights; a lot of my buddies came from single-parent homes and were eventually arrested for armed robbery. One of my good friends was shot and killed in his own driveway. Over time, all that adversity and trauma taught me that I didn't need to lead with the anger I felt in those situations—quite the opposite, actually. So when officers told me I was too nice, I always responded the same way.

"Don't take my kindness as a weakness."

See, I've always seen myself as meek. And there's a difference between *meekness* and *weakness*. Weakness is no strength at all. Meekness is strength under control.

I explained this difference to my kids a while back. We were headed to the zoo, and the whole way there I was hyping my favorite exhibit: the lions.

> Weakness is no strength at all. Meekness is strength under control.

"I love the lions," I told them. "Their roars can be heard over a mile away."

I recited every fact I knew about the kings of the jungle almost as if I was reciting sports statistics from my favorite NFL player. The more I talked, the more it amped my kids.

We arrived at the zoo and made our way to the snakes, the monkeys, the giraffes—everything but the lions. We were saving the best for last.

"Here's the grand finale," I said, just as the sun was going down. "Are you guys ready?"

The near-deafening chorus of "Yeah!" echoed down the paved paths as we rounded a final corner, approached the lion exhibit, and peered in. And…wouldn't you know it? The lions were asleep.

"*Dang*, Dad," my son said. "You've been talking up these lions all day long, but they look like the weakest animal here."

"Mm," I nodded. "They may look weak, but would you want to get in that enclosure with them?"

"NO!"

"Why not?"

My son looked at me like I was crazy. "Because that lion could rip my head off!"

That's exactly what meekness looks like. The lion we observed appeared relaxed, warm and fuzzy—cute, even. But given the opportunity, he could still defend his pride at a moment's notice. He had his strength under control.

When it comes to respect, be the lion. Exercise your strength in such a way that you can stand your ground when needed and keep your emotions in check as you give respect to others.

And, most importantly, respect *yourself*.

To do love, empathy, and respect right, you need to first have them for yourself. To love others, you have to learn how to love yourself. To empathize with others, first learn how to empathize with *you*.

Same goes for respect.

Respect and Disrespect are Two Sides of the Same Price Tag

That day at Valley State Prison, the common denominator that put each man behind bars— his desire for respect—was motivated by something deeper. As I listened to each man tell his story, I was awestruck by a realization: rooted at the heart of every desire for respect was a deep insecurity. "Respect" was the false sense of security they sought to fill a seemingly unfillable hole.

Look—the cost of respect is simple math. When we do the wrong things to develop respect the wrong way, the consequences can be, literally, deadly.

Learning how to battle and win against your insecurities allows you to come across as confident in the person you are (rather than debilitated by the insecurities you feel), and to get there, you first have to be able to respect yourself. But imagine what might have happened if the men at Valley State had allowed their insecurities to become their greatest strengths. What kind of world might that have created?

Throughout my career, I've had the privilege of talking with some of the greatest speakers known to man. And I'm always amazed when one of them says to me, "I don't like public speaking."

Really?

It boggles the mind, but many of these powerful, professional speakers actually have a fear of speaking to large groups of people. And yet, they turned the thing that could have crippled them into their greatest strength. Now the rest of the world gets the benefit.

Is it an Attack on Me?

When Michael Brown was killed in Ferguson, Missouri, the entire city was nearly burned down overnight, and the entire nation was up in arms. Thousands of miles away in Los Angeles, California, people started looking at me…differently. You could even say sideways. When I went out on calls for service, civilians badmouthed me. *ACAB*, they said. *Pig. Uncle Tom*, you name it, I heard it.

Each time someone was controversially killed by the police, it got worse. People were attacking me like crazy. As an officer, it would have been easy to just…react. "Man," I could've said, "why are you coming at me like that? You don't even know who I am." And although that's true, I had to take a step back. Were they attacking me, or were they attacking what I do?

When Jesus was on the cross, He prayed forgiveness over those who had crucified Him. "Father, forgive them," He said, *"for they know not what they do."*

When I looked at my situation through that lens, I could understand that the people who attacked me were reacting from a place of insecurity and weakness. They were angry and afraid, and they were lashing out. That truth didn't make it right that they attacked me. In no way did it justify their actions or mean they shouldn't be held accountable.

But it did prompt a different reaction in me.

Instead of swearing back when people came at me, or angrily detaining and investigating them, I was able to stop, collect myself, and calmly say, "Can I ask you a question? Why are you swearing at me and calling me names? Do you even know who I am?" Each question seemed to peel back another layer, until finally we were at the heart of things.

"I'm sorry," the person would often say. "I didn't mean that."

I see similar situations play out on social media all the time. Remember earlier in this book when I said we seek out those who are like us? There's nothing inherently wrong with that, and yet it sometimes creates situations in which individuals feel free to attack an "other" because they feel supported by their group. Some of these very individuals have followed my social accounts for a long time. Whenever I posted a video that depicted officers using justified force (and explain why it was justified), these followers took it as an invitation to attack me.

At times, I've responded to some of them with some of the same questions I used in the field. In each instance, the fact that I was able to slow down, give grace, and show mercy actually enabled me to build a bridge instead of widening the gap. Over time, I even connected with a few people through direct messaging and built relationships with them over time. I learned that many had lashed out because of something in their past. "I had a bad experience once," they'd say, "and it's why I still feel like this."

They weren't actually attacking me, I realized. Like the men of Valley State, they were reacting to their own insecurities.

When we're under the fire of someone else's disrespect, we must separate the disrespect from ourselves. Take a step back from the situation. Are they really attacking *you*, or is it just their insecurities lashing out? Many times, it's just them dealing with their own stuff.

But.

What if it isn't?

How to Keep from Taking it Personally

Our human nature has greedy hands. It will want to latch on to the attack and take it personally. But I promise you this: that won't help.

Have you heard the old saying, "Do you want to win the battle or the war?" My friend, not every battle is worth being fought. Those social media posts I was just talking about? They were bad. A lot of them came from other officers who more or less created an entire thread devoted to calling me offensive names and saying I wasn't a real cop. They made me really angry, and the situation was uncomfortable for a while.

Thankfully, I had my dad's wisdom to fall back on. "If they're not saying something about you," he'd say, "you're doing something wrong."

I got into law enforcement because I wanted to change the face of modern police work. The pushback and personal attacks were evidence that I was succeeding. I was changing a culture. Contention is a natural part of that process, and it can come from the places you least expect.

In the face of that criticism, I could have given in. I could have given those other officers what they *really* wanted: to get a rise out of me. But if they'd succeeded in pushing me to say slanderous things about them, I would've made the situation far worse. It would have become a very public, very nasty version of my interaction with Adele.

Neither of those battles were worth fighting.

Here's a truth I carry with me every day: when you're doing the right thing, with the right heart, you will meet contention—maybe even from your inner circle. People will misunderstand your motives; they'll criticize or even defame you. But if you can keep your head up, take your lickings, and walk away, you'll never have to worry about that person finding victory over you. They might win a battle or two, but the war will be yours to win.

And, if you stay the course while leading with love, empathy, and respect, you might even win them to your cause.

Leading With Respect is an Intentional Mindset

Being intentional doesn't always come naturally to us. Sometimes, in order to intentionally lead with love, empathy, and respect, we need to force ourselves to do things we don't really want to do.

Like I've said, our emotions play a huge role in this—so huge, that we have to gut-check our initial, natural reactions. Sometimes, our emotional responses are really good. Other times, not so much. But—just like empathy—intentional respect means *authentic* respect. Roll up to someone with fake respect, and they'll see right through you. They'll understand that you're out to get something from them, and that will wreck whatever connection you're working to build.

Intentional respect looks like giving something to a person that they haven't earned (and maybe don't deserve). In practice, *authentic* intentional respect means making up your mind to give grace and mercy—and stand firm on your decision—no matter what. In other words, the Ryan in me doesn't get a say about who gets grace and who doesn't. It's that simple.

Keep in mind, though, that this might feel like it puts you in conflict with your own self-respect. In fact, *expect* to feel this way. Our human natures are powerful; they send out emotional shockwaves capable of shaking us to our core. Many times, that's for good reason. Not every single person on this planet deserves your respect.

But when you come into contact with a person who you truly cannot show authentic, intentional respect, the best thing to do is opt out of having a relationship with them. This doesn't happen to me often, but it does happen. From there, my strategy is to continue to be who I am, and allow myself to shine so brightly that the people I don't respect will see.

It's how I respect us both.

Career Criminal

One night, while I was still a patrol officer, I was at the station booking evidence. It was late; dark out. I was listening to the police radio while I worked and heard that some of my partners had responded to a call. They were dealing with an uncooperative suspect at an apartment building a few miles from the station.

"Officer Tillman," I heard through the radio. "Will you respond and assist at the scene?"

When I arrived, the situation was tense. A shooting had occurred, and my fellow officers believed someone inside the apartment was critically injured—possibly bleeding out—and the original, uncooperative suspect wouldn't budge, refusing to let them in to help.

I recognized the suspect immediately. His name was Shawn, and he had a rap sheet with approximately a hundred arrests from that year alone—several of which I'd made myself. Shawn was a career criminal. After every arrest and brush with the system, he always returned to his illegal activities.

Still, I'd always made it a point to treat him with respect. Despite his criminal activities, we had things in common: we were two Black men around the same age who had come from similar backgrounds. In a lot of ways, he reminded me of friends I grew up with—and that made it easy for me to establish a connection with him.

I walked up to the apartment and started talking. Through that conversation, the other officers and I were able to successfully detain Shawn and gain entry to the apartment. Inside, we found three other people—young guys, like Shawn and me—and learned that what we'd feared was true.

A gunshot victim lay dead on the floor, and no one was willing to talk.

Especially Shawn.

CHAPTER 6

Influence is Relational

S hawn.

We arrested the three young suspects and drove them with Shawn back to our holding facility. At the time, I was still a patrol officer—I hadn't yet been given any special assignments, and I wasn't yet a detective or negotiator. But what I had was the ability to connect with people and really talk with them.

I watched as the detectives attempted to get information out of Shawn. They wanted to know who pulled the trigger on the victim. But Shawn had been in and out of the system so many times, he wasn't playing ball. He refused to give them anything.

After a while, they reemerged from his cell. I overheard them talking about the fact that they weren't getting anywhere and that none of the other suspects were willing to talk either.

"Hey Ryan," one of the detectives said. "You had a rapport with Shawn at the scene. Why don't you try and go talk to him?"

I agreed, and I walked into his cell.

Shawn was hungry, so I made sure someone brought him and the others a meal. He was cold, too—they all were—so we gave them what they needed to warm up. Finally, I sat down with him to talk. Not officer-to-suspect, but person-to-person.

It was almost like having a conversation with one of my homies from my old neighborhood.

"Look, man," I said. "With everything that's going on right now, everyone thinks you did it. It's possible to assume one of the other guys pulled the trigger. But at the end of the day, they don't have a rap sheet like you do. They weren't the ones being uncooperative and refusing to come out of the house, and they haven't been arrested multiple times. This situation isn't going to play out in your favor.

"We need to know who did it," I continued. "If it wasn't you, man…I know you don't want to be a snitch. But at the very least, you need to give me something because there's going to be a time when you look back and wonder if you made the right decision, whatever that decision is. The choice is yours."

I stood up, ready to walk out. I got as far as opening the door to leave.

"Hey, Tillman," Shawn said. "I want to talk to you."

I shut the door and turned around. "You have my word that I'll keep everything a secret as much as I can for now. I'll treat you like a man. I'm not going to disrespect you, but I do want you to be honest with me."

And he was. Shawn identified the shooter—one of the other individuals in the apartment—and we were able to close the case.

Here's the thing. Why would a career criminal have given up that kind of information? Sure, you can say he was in it for himself—he didn't want to go down for a crime he didn't commit, especially if that crime was homicide, or even murder. He was saving his own skin. But if that was true, why didn't Shawn tell the detectives right away? Why did everything change when I got involved?

In all transparency, I wasn't inside Shawn's head, so I can't answer that. But what I can tell you is that I'd developed a relationship with

Shawn long before that moment. And with every encounter, detainment, and arrest, I chose to make investments in that relationship.

Over and over again, I treated Shawn with the kind of respect I would show to any person. I didn't let it keep me from doing my job, of course, but I always made sure Shawn knew that when I arrived on the scene, he could trust me to be fair, honest, and kind.

And, at the end of the day, I believe our relationship changed everything.

Why Relationships Matter

Relationships do not all look the same. They don't all carry the same weight or hold the same level of intensity. In fact, "having a relationship" doesn't necessarily mean "being friends" and spending lots of time hanging out with every person who crosses your path. It can be as simple as always saying hello to the barista who makes your morning drink at Starbucks, calling them by name, and asking how their day is going. And even the smallest relationships you form share a common thread: they will add so much opportunity, meaning, and purpose to your life.

My whole life, I heard my dad say, "It's not what; it's who." I never understood that when I was younger, but by the time I reached high school and college, it started to sink in. I was already forming relationships with people who would open doors in my life, and that proximity got me into rooms I never knew existed—or could have even imagined.

Here's a simple fact: we don't have access to every door on this planet, *but someone else does.* The authentic relationships we form give us opportunities to learn about what's behind them as we naturally build trust together. That's what happened with Shawn—the relationship we established opened a door I would never have been able to access otherwise.

You may be reading this book and thinking, *Okay, Ryan, that's amazing. But I'm not a police officer—how does this apply to my life?* I hear you. What I'll say is that my experience with Shawn speaks to something deeper: how relationships bring the unobtainable within our reach.

Before I go any farther, we need to pause. I want to make it perfectly clear that *I am not talking about using people to get what you want or to go where you want to go.* When I say connection is about people and proximity, I am talking about developing authentic relationships for the sake of the relationship alone. I've already said this, but it's important enough to say again: making relationships for the sake of rewards *will not work*. Sure, it might get you where you planned to go. But it won't open the doors you never thought you could reach.

> **Making relationships for the sake of rewards *will not work*. Sure, it might get you where you planned to go. But it won't open the doors you never thought you could reach.**

All right. Unpause.

When I was younger, I viewed certain things as unreachable. For example, earning a hundred thousand dollars a year seemed crazy hard—like something I could never do. But over time, I began meeting more and more people who made that salary. As our relationships grew, so did my understanding about their means and income. I learned that making a hundred thousand a year wasn't nearly as difficult as I'd thought, and before long, my own salary surpassed that amount. Now, I find myself in rooms and becoming friends with millionaires and billionaires. Each relationship increases my exposure to how that kind of wealth is made.

It isn't about money, though. In fact, you could substitute "income" in that example with just about anything else, and the logic holds. That's because relationships teach us that people are people, no matter what. The difference between average and great isn't some magical, unattainable it-factor. Greatness comes from relating—and doing just a little bit more.

One More For the Good

Notice I said, "a little bit," and not "a huge amount." Does that surprise you? When I learned it, it surprised me. I had always subscribed to the common misconception that says, "To be *great*, I have to do much, much more than the average person." But that's simply not true. We just need to take one more step than everyone else.

I began putting that mindset into practice back in high school, which ultimately got me a full scholarship after I walked-on to the football team at the University of Nevada, Las Vegas. Before that happened, I was one of the smallest guys on the team. I had a solid work ethic, but I struggled to gain weight.

One day I decided to approach my training in a different way. Every time the coach told us to do ten reps, I did eleven. If he told us to run 400 yards, I ran 500. The thing is, I didn't have to do double or triple of what everyone else did. That small, incremental effort was enough. I stood out.

I continued to bring that forward in my life.

In my early days as a police officer, my department received notification that someone had been shoplifting from a local Kohl's department store. The suspect had a very specific system: he would go into the store, fill a cart with expensive merchandise, and then switch the price tags for ones with lower amounts. He would go through the check-out like anyone else and watch as the items rang up for far less than they should have. Then he'd pay and walk out the front door. He had been at it for a while.

The store's loss prevention department eventually caught on to what he was doing. By their calculations, he had stolen over a thousand dollars' worth of merchandise, which officially classified his crime as grand theft. Their parking lot cameras had caught the suspect getting in and out of his car, and they had his license plate number.

Normally in these situations, a patrol officer (like I was at the time) would be tasked with going to the scene, taking the initial report, submitting it, and then allowing the detective bureau to follow up. But my department had always encouraged us to take on the investigations ourselves. I saw the opportunity to do a little bit more in this instance. So, after taking the initial report, I returned to the station and did a workup on the license plate.

I learned a lot. The plates were registered to a man named Ivan. After digging a little deeper into his background, I discovered he had run the scam multiple times and stolen tens of thousands of dollars' worth of merchandise.

I worked with the detective bureau and put together a search warrant, and we went to Ivan's house. We executed the search and found the stolen goods *and* all of the materials and equipment he was using to print fake price tags with functional barcodes. When the search was over, we arrested Ivan for grand theft.

By now, you know me well enough to know I didn't just read Ivan his rights and deposit him at the jail. I took the next step and began a conversation. We talked, and I learned about his life. From the outside looking in, Ivan seemed like a decent, well-put-together guy. But underneath it all, he was struggling. His finances were in trouble and his marriage had soured. All the theft was an attempt to live life as someone else and cover the trouble he was in.

As we continued talking, I developed a relationship with Ivan that day—not a long-term, abiding friendship, but one that allowed me to pray with him and let him know I would continue to remember him in my prayers.

Fast forward six months to the day I crossed paths with Ivan in the city after he'd gotten out of jail.

"Ryan, I just want to thank you," he said. "You really put things in perspective for me that day. I was spiraling and I needed to get caught."

"Yeah?"

"Yeah. The grace and mercy you showed me—it really helped me get back on my feet."

If I had to guess, I'd say no number of *things* would have unlocked the door to redemption that barred Ivan's way forward. I mean, think about it: money might have cleared up his financial misfortune for a while, but would it have restored his relationship with his wife, or address any of the root causes of the issues Ivan faced? Likely not.

Ivan simply needed *connection*. He needed to be seen, exactly as he was, and held accountable with mercy and grace. He needed someone in his path to open doors he couldn't open on his own.

"Do a little more" was the ethos I brought to my investigation of Ivan, and that work was part of the reason I won one of law enforcement's most prestigious awards: Officer of the Year. I had only been an officer for about eighteen months, and I remember being pretty blown away when they told me. I didn't feel like I'd done much—I'd simply followed a couple of leads in Ivan's investigation and others like it, and followed my heart to create *Breaking Barriers United*, an organization that was formed to bridge the gap between law enforcement and the community. Doing just one more thing than the average person put me in a different category. Again.

Although awards are great, and I feel honored and humbled to have received the Officer of the Year honor, when I look back at the situation that brought it about, I can see what came from it was something much richer than recognition. The little bit more I did in the investigation became an interaction, and that interaction blossomed into a relationship that influenced change in Ivan's life. It stopped his spiral, and that meant people in his community were no longer being taken advantage of.

Just take a moment to let that sink in. One relationship, as small as it was, changed *so much*. Now, I bring this approach to everything I do in life. It's the origin of my organization, *One More for the Good*. In life there will always be requirements, when you do a little more than what is required (one more for the good), it will push you from ordinary to extraordinary without overexertion. I want everyone to see that pushing yourself just a little further than everyone else will automatically put you ahead.

And that kind of effort can change the world.

Service Before Self

How we make others feel is especially important in today's technology-dominated world. Social media is turning us into one of the most depressed generations to ever exist. We scroll, scroll, scroll through our social media feeds, and our thoughts swirl around what we don't have or haven't done. *They're traveling again*, we think. *Why don't I get to do that?*

The saddest part is that these thoughts—and the feelings of inadequacy that come with them—cause us to forget the true blessings we have in our own lives. The best way to counter that in our culture is to put others before ourselves.

Just think about it. What might happen when *I'm not good enough* becomes *How can I help you?* When *I don't have enough* becomes *What can I do for you?*

My friend, I'll tell you from experience: we get our confidence back. We get our gratitude back. We get motivated to go out and help others again. We've all heard it said that "giving is contagious," and it's true—but it's also more than that. The Bible tells us that when we give to others by returning ten percent of our earnings to God, we increase our blessings by tenfold.

INFLUENCE IS RELATIONAL

When it comes to serving others, we're all familiar with one of the best examples in business. I bring this up at my presentations all the time, actually. "Show of hands," I say. "How many of you have ever had bad service at Chick-fil-A?" No one raises their hands.

What's interesting is that there are other restaurants that serve chicken that is arguably just as good or better than Chick-fil-A's, but Chick-fil-A is the only restaurant with lines of cars wrapped around the restaurant (and sometimes down the street). Why is that?

It isn't about the chicken.

When we emphasize service before self, what we're really doing is saying to another person, "I see you. I care about you, and you matter." Consistently make someone feel good about themselves, and they'll keep coming back for more.

The way Chick-fil-A's employees conduct themselves reminds me of a widow who gave all the money she had to her church. Biblical accounts in Mark and Luke tell us it wasn't a lot of money—hers was the smallest donation by far, actually—but she gave it without holding back. In that one act of sacrifice, her heart gave everything, too. In turn, God blessed her beyond measure.

And He does the same for us.

Putting others before ourselves sometimes means we yield things that aren't easy to give up. Sacrifice is hard, or it wouldn't be called sacrifice. But that time, that energy, that money, that food you feel like you can't spare will be multiplied into blessings and goodness we can't possibly imagine or foresee.

The Domino Effects of Your Efforts Today

I always tell people that every time we have a relationship with someone, we're making a positive or negative investment. In turn, that investment becomes momentum. It's like lining up enough dominos to fill a gymnasium, and toppling them all with the momentum of a single push. We never know how far the effects of one action will spread.

In relationships, there's no way of knowing how far our investments will go. I never would have guessed that investing respect into a relationship with Shawn would have resulted in him one day helping me close a homicide case. I was lucky that day. Many times, we never actually see the return on our investment in others.

But that can be a good thing if it means our investment has grown legs and just keeps going.

When I was in middle school, I had a group of coaches—Coach Anthony Brown, Coach Brian Harper, Coach Rubin, and Coach Greg Watson—who taught me a lot about football, but even more about life. When I got to high school, they continued coaching our football team (all the way to an undefeated record our freshman year, I might add) through my senior year, while doing their normal jobs as campus safety officers. We developed great relationships, and they had a significant influence over my life.

Fast forward fifteen years or so, and Anthony is still a big part of my life. A lot of the lessons I learned from him allowed me to give back. He taught me so much about coaching, about personal development, and about investing in others that I've been able to pass on to a tremendous amount of people that he'll never know. His investment in me was the push that knocked over that first domino, and we're still learning how big the gymnasium is.

We've seen this happen before at an even bigger scale, of course. Think about Martin Luther King Jr. Think about Nelson Mandela. Whose investment toppled the first domino in their chain of influence? Or think about the widow in the Bible. Her gift to God—her investment in people—is still changing hearts and minds.

Thousands of years later.

The Difference We Make

Earlier, I mentioned that when we tap into people, give them resources, and have succeeded in being the most authentic version of ourselves, it brings us closer to fulfilling our purpose in life. Let's dig into that.

When I meet people, many of them address me as "Officer Ryan" or "Officer Tillman." After getting to know them, I always change that. "Hey, you don't have to call me 'officer,'" I'll say. "Call me Ryan."

Titles are important—whether you're an officer or the chief of police or have a doctorate, you've earned that distinction. But the reason I ask people to call me by my first name is because it reminds me that my title—police officer—is not who I am. It's just what I do.

See the difference? It's an important thing to keep in perspective because it helps us avoid a common trap. So many of us get a job and allow that job to define us. We allow our titles to overshadow who we are as a person, and that makes it very difficult to develop relationships. Our interactions come off as if they're hierarchical—as if we're talking down to anyone who isn't at "our level."

But the truth is, we're all just people with emotions and experiences—even the guy who's higher up the ladder than we are.

Every chief I've ever had at my department has had an open-door policy. But nine times out of ten, the line-level workers didn't use it. "Who wants to talk to their boss?" is a common sentiment.

The thing is, it's really important to have a genuine relationship with the person who's leading the ship. Stopping in and saying hello will help me learn what kind of person they are, what they want from the organization (and me). It will help me gauge whether I'm doing the things I'm supposed to be doing, too.

Plus, a simple "hello" is what they want, too.

I learned this from my own chief. "Ryan," she said, "the hard thing about my position is that when you're walking the hallways, everybody has to say 'hi.'"

My chief meant that it was impossible to know if her staff and team genuinely liked or cared about her. They were going to say hello regardless, simply because of her status. And like any boss, supervisor, or CEO, she longed for someone to come and talk to her. She wanted relationships with her team—not sucking up or butt-kissing to get a promotion, but the same kind of connection that every human needs.

I make an effort to stop in and say hello to the chief because I want them to know that even though I recognize their status, I see them as a good person first. Doing so helps me tap into the bigger purpose we all have on this earth: being a connector of people and making them feel seen.

I once read a true story in a devotional Bible that stuck with me. A man had written a suicide note that said, "Today I'm going to walk down to the Golden Gate Bridge. If no one says hello to me by the time I get there, I'm going to jump."

Hello is that simple, that powerful. In this instance, just one utterance of the word would have literally saved the life of an individual who was hurting. Because he did jump, and he did die, and it didn't have to be that way.

A little bit more in the way of a relationship could have changed everything.

CHAPTER 7

Transformation

Ryan. George Floyd's killing brought this country into one of its darkest hours. As a police officer, I was in the thick of things: attacks on law enforcement; protests; arguments about morals, ethics, and race. All across the nation, people were taking a knee in solidarity with George Floyd, who died after Officer Derek Chauvin knelt on his neck for more than eight minutes.

In particular, those demonstrations divided law enforcement. Some departments refused to take a knee and be exploited by the media and other groups who insisted on painting all cops as racist killers. Other departments saw taking a knee as an act of solidarity—an opportunity to acknowledge that what had happened to George was simply not right.

Personally, I felt that what happened to him was wrong on all accounts, and almost immediately after his death I made a video about the oath police officers are sworn to uphold. The moment Derek Chauvin did what he did, I believe that oath was compromised. My video went viral. It wasn't long before people started asking me if *I* would take a knee if everyone else around me did.

"Heck no," I answered. "I'm not about to take a knee. I'm not about to pander to the community and make it seem like I'm the person who did something wrong."

At the time, I had no way of knowing just how my words and resolve were about to be tested.

The very next day, my department got word of a protest on its way to our front yard. Hundreds, maybe thousands of people were marching from the opposite end of the city, headed straight for us. They planned to hold a rally in front of our department.

Given what was happening all around us and across the country, we had already prepared for something like this. "It's going to get here, and it's going to be what it is," we said. "We just have to handle it."

Still, a lot of officers were uneasy—and rightfully so. It was impossible to know the outcome of a protest of that magnitude. We didn't know how many people with inflammatory views might show up; we had no idea what else to expect. The situation might very well be a ticking time bomb counting down to chaos.

Our plan was to remain inside the building, allow the protest to happen, and be ready for the unexpected. We didn't want to provoke tempers or violence by being outside. But my boss pulled me and one other officer aside. "Ryan," he said, "if something goes crazy, the two of you are going to go out there and see if you can de-escalate."

"OK."

We slipped outside to listen. People were angry and up in arms, but they protested peacefully. But the longer it went on, the more nervous I became. I knew it was likely that someone at that protest would take a knee.

"Lord, please," I prayed, "please don't let this happen. If I take a knee, I'll be an outcast in my department. Most of them already think I'm a double agent as it is."

The protesters continued to chant, and I continued to pray.

I had two revelations. The first was this. When I proposed to my beautiful wife, I did it because I knew that I was ready to marry her. I got down on one knee because it was an outward way to demonstrate my willingness to serve her needs and put them before my own for the rest of my life, even in the times I didn't want to.

The second revelation was one about Jesus. When He was with His disciples right before going to be crucified, He got down on one knee and washed the dust and grime from their feet. *This is the king of all kings*, I thought. *The person who is God.* He didn't hesitate to kneel before His own disciples in an act of servitude.

In that moment, I knew God was reminding me that I wasn't there to be served, right, or prideful. I was an officer because He had first called me to serve. *If that moment comes*, I heard in my heart, *I want to see how you'll respond.* Sure enough, I heard a call ring out across the protest.

"For the next eight minutes, we're going to take a knee in solidarity with George Floyd."

Transformation is an Inward-Out Process

Oh my goodness, I thought. *I don't want to do this.*

But I was, and remain, a public *servant*. That is the call on my life.

So, my friends, I took a knee.

I didn't do it for all the reasons everyone else did. I didn't do it to pander to the masses or because they'd gotten the better of me and forced me to do it because I was a public servant. I did it because the Holy Spirit instructed me to do what Jesus did and what I had done for my wife. *When you take a knee*, the Holy Spirit spoke to my heart, *do it as an outward expression of your willingness to serve them.*

The thing is, sometimes transformation causes us to go to unexpected places. Sometimes it causes us to see things through a different lens.

I'd been looking at it through the lens of law enforcement. I'd viewed it through a "media capitalizing on a terrible event" lens. Both of those were *outward* perspectives, and they were telling me "Don't do it." If God hadn't shown me how to turn inward and see it from His perspective, the outcome would've been completely different.

Get Comfortable Being Uncomfortable

I'm going to be totally transparent here. In the moment, as I looked around and saw all the other officers who were still standing, kneeling felt *so weird*—as weird as it was to go back to Gary's house that day and pray with his wife and kids. I was wildly uncomfortable. At the same time, I recognized that obedience as a way to lay down my pride. My Heavenly Father had asked me to do this, and I realized that because of that calling, I didn't mind it at all.

I took a lot of heat from other police officers, and I did my best to explain why I'd done it. Some understood, others didn't. But that was also when I saw so many people in the community come alongside me. It was empathy on display. And through it, I was personally transformed.

I'd been a public servant for a while, but that was the first time I truly understood what public servitude is. It is the ability to acknowledge my personal wrongs, or the wrongs of my profession, when we mess up. It is being able to drop my pride so I can think and hear the community's needs before my own. And sometimes, it is making the unpopular choice, or maybe even losing your life to save another (like Jesus did).

Personal transformation often requires that we go against the grain and do what no one else wants—or is willing—to do. That's why it also requires personal conviction—so we aren't led astray by the outside voices that will drown out the small, still voice of the Holy Spirit if we let them. It takes effort to stay the course and continue to die to our human natures.

It's not a comfortable experience, but growth never is. Real transformation requires us to submerge ourselves in uncomfortable environments and, well, get comfortable there. But take heart. Every time I've challenged and pushed myself to go to places I first resisted, I come out on the other side and say, "You know what? It wasn't that bad."

> **Personal transformation often requires that we go against the grain and do what no one else wants—or is willing—to do.**

That happened recently. I was on retreat with Kimberly and some of the other couples in leadership at our church. One evening, we were sitting out by the pool, where one of my really good friends kept pressing me to jump in.

Let me tell you that I am *not* a cold pool water person. Give me a hot jacuzzi in a chilly environment all day long, but I don't want it the other way around. I won't even swim on a hot day.

"Heck no," I said. "That water is freezing."

"Man," he said. "Just *do* it."

Normally I would never get talked into anything—let alone jumping into an ice-cold pool—but this time, I dutifully toed up to the water's edge. Across the pool, our wives got their cameras out.

I leapt.

The shock on my body was intense, but I swam all the way to the other side and jumped straight into the jacuzzi to warm back up. Before long, we were all cracking up. I noticed that there was another guy in our group who hadn't jumped the first time, and I honed in.

"C'mon, man," I said. "Let's go jump. If you do it, I'll do it again."

We did, and we all shared another moment of laughter and community.

So ask yourself: what might a little discomfort be worth to you? Is the risk worth the reward? Because, look—there is almost always a reward, and usually the worst that can happen pales in comparison. In my life, I've seen new and restored relationships, financial increase, and personal development. Getting connected with Oprah and becoming good friends with Dak grew out of the moment of discomfort I experienced while taking a knee.

And by the way—that second leap into the pool? It wasn't nearly as bad as the first. Every leap of faith makes the next one a little easier.

Transformation: From Self to Kingdom

You may be holding this book and thinking of transformations you'd like to see in your own profession or organization. I think that's great. Just keep in mind that if you want to make the change there, you first have to do the work to transform yourself. It can't happen in reverse.

Transformation is a pattern of growth. Personal transformation gives you the kind of credibility to propose solutions within organizations. That's because when people see the thing you've recommended playing out in your life, they know it's sincere. There's no ulterior motive attached to what you're trying to do.

We all know what the opposite of that looks like—we've seen that person and how they operate. And we aren't surprised when every solution they bring to the table benefits them more than anyone else.

But when you have a reputation for putting others before yourself, the recommendations you make carry a different weight. People who have seen your heart for making their lives better will want to be around you, so they can experience transformation, too. Transformation is infectious that way. And it will ultimately impact your organization.

A good friend of mine recently visited the company headquarters of Chick-fil-A. While there, he ate a meal with some employees in the company cafeteria. One of them introduced my friend to a Chick-fil-A executive—someone who not only had huge stature within the organization, but was also a member of the family that started the company.

This executive treated my friend like royalty. He put his own meal aside so he could focus on speaking with my friend and learning all about him. When my friend finished his meal, the guy even threw away his trash. His actions demonstrated his true servant mentality—a mindset that undoubtedly benefited his organization.

And we see that executive's willingness to serve rippling outward into our own communities, right? I've already talked about the ways Chick-fil-A's service has resulted in booming business. But let's make that personal. How many new stores have popped up in your town? How many jobs have been created in your neighborhood? How many practical circumstances have improved as a result, and for how many people? How many times has a smile changed your day? And how might that pattern of growth and abundance inspire us to change our perspectives?

The goal of transformation—and the end result, if we're faithful—is to see the world through a Kingdom lens. When that happens, we get clarity. God's plans become visible to us as we gain understanding and insight about His movements in and through our daily lives.

When my dad died, I used to wonder all the time why he had to go through such pain. Why did *he* have to be the one bedridden with MS? Why did he have to suffer? Through my earthly eyes, it seemed random, senseless, and unnecessarily cruel. But viewing the situation through a Kingdom lens brought everything into focus. My dad's experience with severe illness taught my family the peace that passes all understanding. If others see that in us and desire to experience it for themselves, then what my dad went through—as painful as it was—was worth it.

If we allow it, God can turn every bad thing into good as long as we love Him and live in His purpose for our lives. But that's hard to see if we're looking through our earthly eyes. So, go ahead. Do the work of transformation, and keep doing it until you're viewing the world from a Kingdom lens—the way I did when I had to take a knee.

If I hadn't done that, you would not be holding this book today. But because I did, I saw my life clearly. None of it was about me, and that's honestly wonderful. Becoming all things to all people means it can't be about me.

CHAPTER 8

Your Legacy is Now

Dig Deep

Becoming all things to all people often means choosing to see the best in them, even when that feels like an impossible task. (As I've said, it doesn't always mean befriending a person. It *can* mean that, but it doesn't have to.) As I shared in the introduction, choosing to see the best in a person will take some extra digging — and I hope this book has demonstrated how I have had to do this in my lifetime. Uncovering that "best" is the map that will allow you to lead with love, empathy, and respect in ways you never have before.

That is especially important when we encounter people who seem entirely unredeemable. My line of work sometimes brings me into contact with adults who have molested children. Their crimes are horrifying, full stop. Nothing—absolutely nothing—justifies what they've done. And yet, when we dig deep enough, we find over and over that they do the things they do because they've spent their entire lives suffocating under the weight of their own trauma.

Like I said, that doesn't justify their actions. It doesn't mitigate the anger we feel toward them—and that's OK. But if we don't try to see some sort of good in *all* people, at what point do we, as a society and as individuals, simply…break?

This chapter is about legacy, and all the ways we are already creating our own. We'll get to the creation part in a minute. For now, take a second to consider that we are capable of leaving behind a legacy of good *or* a legacy of harm.

Peeling back the layers of trauma for a person who doesn't seem to deserve our compassion can go a long way to help them heal. We might even see that they're just someone who was dealt a bad hand and left to endure their hurt alone.

I'm not saying that's easy. Straight up—it isn't. But when we can give of our own goodness to help someone who needs it most, even (or especially) when it's undeserved, we might hand them the tool they need to break the cycle of their life.

When we choose to put on a set of Happy Eyes, we truly have the power to change someone else's reality for the better. We can change the course of another person's legacy just by choosing to see the best in others. And in a world that's full of so much negativity and heartbreak, don't we all want that? Don't we all need a way to go out and create happiness for ourselves and others?

Bigger Than Anything—For Someone Else

Learning how to love people allows us to overlook hurts and slights. In the absence of those things, we can begin to heal, and even gain a newfound respect for one another. My mom taught me that. She showed me that love covers a multitude of sins. When I made mistakes, I knew that no matter what I'd done, I wouldn't lose her love. It was—and always will be—abiding.

And I am a result of that legacy.

See, leading with love, empathy, and respect begins in the home. It has the power to preserve families; it can heal the brokenness that causes generational trauma. It is bigger than anything we do in this world.

Growing up, my mom was always my home. I knew that wherever she was, I could go there and feel comfortable. I'll never forget the time she helped me when my friend and I needed to find a new apartment. "Go look," she instructed, "and tell me what you find."

At one place in particular, the woman giving us a tour followed us everywhere we went. It was a little weird, but I tried to brush it off—until she said, "You know you guys can't afford to live here, right?"

At this point, she didn't know anything about us—including the state of our finances. She was making assumptions. For the first time in my life, I was really hurt by that special brand of disrespect. *How could you say that about us*, I thought, *when you don't even know us?*

I called my mom. She reassured me that she and my dad would help us get where we needed to go, and then said the words I'll always remember.

"Unfortunately, there will be people in your life who are like this—who judge you without knowing anything about you. But as long as you know who you are, that's all that matters. So, let this be a lesson: what a person says about you is not reality. Only you control that."

Now, I'm fortunate enough to have that kind of support with Kimberly, too. When the world beats us down, we all need that person we can go to. And. We also should strive to be that person for someone else.

Every School Has a Name

I challenge you to take a snapshot of your life. If you left this world today, what would your obituary say? If you're not sure, or you don't like what's coming to mind right now, it's time to get to work.

Think of it way: every school has a name. And not just any name, but the name of someone who brought positive change to the school and its community. That person went out and did something that was big and bright enough to carve their name in history.

It's unlikely that Martin Luther King Jr. or Caesar Chavez started their day by wondering how many schools would eventually be named after them. They simply experienced the process of growth that comes from living a life of love, empathy, and respect. They stuck with personal transformation and followed it through, to the point that their legacies transformed our nation, maybe even the world. The recognition they received was just a byproduct of each and every act of service they performed.

I'm not suggesting that anyone abandon their goals to focus solely on the here and now. What I'm asking is that we all choose to live lives that are so written over with love, empathy, and respect, that we can sit down when it's all said and done and look back without regret.

Look—how many of us are living our lives because someone else wants to act a certain way? How many decisions are we making on a day-to-day basis because of someone else's expectations? We should take others' expectations into consideration from time to time. But if it's up to me, I would rather die knowing that I took a knee because it's what God wanted me to do than not take a knee because everyone else told me not to.

The reality is this. If we try to live up to everyone else's expectations, we never will, and the sheer impossibility of trying will make us miserable. But courageously and deeply expressing the vulnerability it takes to lead with love, empathy, and respect can only lead us to the life we're meant to live.

At the end of the day, if we do what we're called or created to do, we will lead lives of minimal regret. And, when we draw our last breath, I truly believe we'll enter the Kingdom of Heaven and hear the words, "Well done, my good and faithful servant."

The Choice is Yours

So, back to that obituary. What is your legacy? How will it live on through others?

My Happy Eyes are an intentional choice. Every morning I wake up and choose to see the best in people, choose to make the most of the hours that lie ahead, choose to love the people in my community. My sisters Lauren and Erin have always said I'm just like my dad—they even call me Earl Tillman Jr. I love that. It's all of the lessons he taught and the stories he told, living through me. And I hope that when I'm gone, those lessons will live on through my kids, Grayson, Gavin, and Ryland.

One way or another, each and every one of us will leave a legacy—good, bad, or somewhere in between. And whether we realize it, we're living that legacy *now*. With every decision, every action, every word, we impact those around us in real time.

It goes without saying, but I'll say it anyway: we don't live in a perfect world. Systems, communities, and families break down. We break down. Imperfect people will never create perfect, failproof systems.

Thankfully, we have the beautiful, perfect example of love, empathy, and respect that Jesus set. We might still experience suffering, but pain and heartache need not be meaningless. They don't have to be what we give to our families, our coworkers, our friends.

They don't have to become our legacy.

Our legacies are ours to choose and shape as we will. So, my friend, my question to you is simple. *What will cause you to smile when it seems there's nothing worth smiling for?*

Will you choose to live with Happy Eyes? Will you lead with love, empathy, and respect? I hope so, because it will help change your life. And it is an absolute necessity if we want to transform our organizations and communities and see the world through a Kingdom lens.

My love for God, my wife, my children, my mom, my sisters, and all my family members and friends, is what allows me to smile without smiling. My hope is that my Happy Eyes are my legacy—one that will inspire you to view your own life in a way that keeps that legacy going.

The Comeback

Remember Gary? Well, fast-forward three months from that day in his living room. My family and I were headed to LAX—one of the busiest airports in the U.S.—to catch a flight to Hawaii. We had two young children at the time. In my infinite wisdom, I'd suggested that we spend the night before our flight at her mother's house—and leave for the airport an hour and a half before our flight.

Yep. I can feel everyone who's ever flown through LAX absolutely cringing right now. Leaving an hour and a half before our flight was *not* the right plan.

The minutes slipped away from me as we inched along the freeway. I started sweating bullets. *This is going to be very, very close*, I thought. Kimberly knew it too, but she wasn't holding it over my head yet. But then we pulled into the serpentine line of cars making their way to the airport, and the tension started closing in on me.

We were still in the car, and our flight was scheduled to take off in thirty minutes.

My friend who had driven us to the airport finally dropped us off at the curb in front of our airline check-in. We clambered inside with all our luggage as fast as we possibly could. With all our bags and kids and strollers, it felt like a scene from *Home Alone*.

Inside, we were met with the sight of another massive, snaking line. We took our place at the back, but I knew we were done for. No way were we making it to the counter, through airport security, and all the way to our gate in time to make our plane.

Out of nowhere, somebody recognized me. I didn't recognize him, but that's not uncommon. Because of my social media presence, I do get recognized pretty frequently.

"Hey, man," I said. "It's good seeing you. Thank you for everything. I have to go check my luggage and find my family, but I'll be back."

"Officer Tillman," he said, "are you running late?"

The guy told me he worked for the airline—the same one we were supposed to be flying with. Despite the time crunch, I stopped to hear him out. I hadn't recognized him before, but now I took a second look, and I *did* remember him. But from where?

Oh, wow, I thought. *It's Gary.*

Gary hurried us to the front of the check-in line and said something to the ticket agent while motioning for Kimberly and the kids to go ahead and go through security. I'd meet them there with our boarding passes, he said, and within minutes they were in my hand.

Suddenly, it was *Home Alone* all over again. But with Gary's help, we bypassed the entire line and quickly got through security—even when TSA personnel questioned us about our strollers.

"You guys have to rush," Gary said. "Where are you going?"

"Hawaii," we answered. In a flash, he loaded our things on a cart and drove us to our gate. It was practically deserted. Everyone else had already boarded. We rushed down the jetway; the same instant our butts hit our seats, the flight lifted off.

A little breathless, Kimberly looked over at me. "How did you know that guy down there?"

I thought of the day I'd been to Gary's house. The pivotal moment we'd navigated together. His family, holding together as best they could in the face of the unimaginable.

I'd given Gary what he needed in that moment. I'd shown him love, empathy, and respect. Little had I known at the time how much I would need those same things in return three months later—or that they would come from the same guy I'd arrested.

"Honey," I said, "get ready. You are *never* going to believe this story."

Afterword

Sometimes I wonder if it is worth the effort—or as I hear so often today, "Is the juice worth the squeeze?" For over forty years I have been lecturing to law enforcement people from around the world. Through education and experience, I have learned quite a bit and I try to share it with law enforcement personnel with the ultimate goal of improving the quality of law enforcement personnel which in turn will ultimately benefit the respective communities they serve.

As I look at the scores of cops doing bad things around our nation, I become frustrated and wonder if anyone is listening to my lectures. This frustration has caused me to put the cops in my various lectures into three categories. Give me a hundred cops in a room and I know that ten of them don't want to be there. In their mind this mandatory training is worthless and a waste of their time. The second category is much larger: eighty-five of them are good people who will do what they are told. They go to the class and try to leave with something beneficial to them.

But then there are the "five-percenters"—the five out of a hundred who want to change the world, who want to make things better, who want to make excellence the norm and not the deviation. My goal for most of the forty-plus years I have been doing this work is to identify the "five percent" and thank them for their work and give them some guidance through books and websites where they can further improve the quality of their work—and hopefully encourage others to get better and better at what they do.

All of this brings me to 2016 when I stood in front of thirty-five cops at the Cavenaugh DUI school in Laguna Niguel, California. Mr. Cavenaugh has a five-day program on how to successfully recognize and arrest people who are under the influence—and I have been the Friday morning "wrap up" presenter in that program for over thirty years. My program is three hours long, with two ten-minute breaks.

At 9:00 we took a break and a very, very young attendee came up to me and asked if he could ask me a question. "Of course," I tell him. He proceeds to ask me a question way, way, way over what is typical for his young age—frankly a brilliant, well thought out question. I tried to answer it the best I could, and we had a brief, but thoughtful conversation. After another hour of lecturing, we took our second break and the same young officer came up to ask a second question—again way, way over his young age and time on the job.

There are time constraints on the breaks so I wrapped up my chat with him by asking, "I want to continue this conversation—is there any way you can come over to my home someday for further discussions?" His "eyes" lit up (I did not know they were *Happy Eyes* at that moment), and he started coming over to my home where we had some serious discussions. I quickly formed the opinion that I was talking to someone very, very special—not just a "five percenter," but someone who really wanted to change the world of law enforcement.

As you might have guessed by now, that young officer was Ryan Tillman. We now close in on almost a decade of conversations. I have had the absolute honor to know Ryan Tillman, his lovely Bride Kimberly, and their three great children and watched him changing the world of law enforcement in America. Between his "Breaking Barriers United" work, and his "It's Needed" conferences, and the hundreds of programs he has with law enforcement officials, community members, students, and other people involved in the criminal justice system, I have learned that he is an "American Treasure."

AFTERWORD

The title of Ryan's book initially fooled me, but after reading the Foreword by Mr. Prescott and the thoughtful dedication and the Introduction…"I got it." Ryan is a very special man who uses his "eyes" to constantly look for the good in people—all people—even the "old white guy" wrapping up the DUI program eight years ago.

Looking into the future, I sense that "brain scans" will be part of the hiring process in law enforcement. I don't know how these "scans" will work exactly, but in talking to the Founder of CORDICO (a mental health and wellness company), Dr. David Black, I further explored this possibility and how it would work. Dr. Black asked me, "What one quality would you want to see in a police officer through this scan?" My brain instantly defaulted to "integrity", but I have learned not to lock myself into something without further consideration.

As our conversation continued, it became obvious to me that my first "mandatory trait" was important (we need cops with integrity!), but more important was "EMPATHY"—having the ability to look at someone and put yourself in their shoes at that moment and understand what is going on in their world and why they are doing what they do. As you read this book you notice that Ryan emphasizes the importance of "empathy" and throughout the book he gives several examples of why this is so, so important. The book is a quick read, but—as with so many quick reads—it will require multiple "rereads" because there is a very important message behind the words in this book. I recently had the opportunity to introduce Ryan to a high-level executive at a national organization. After the introduction, this executive called me back with this comment: "Ryan is the 'real deal' – who practices his preaching, and he gets it!"

Please enjoy reading (and re-reading) this book and recognize that if we had more people like Ryan and Kimberly our world would be a much better place.

—Gordon Graham, Co-founder of *Lexipol* and former Commander California Highway Patrol

About the Author

Ryan Tillman is currently a Police Officer for the Chino Police Department as well as the CEO and founder of Breaking Barriers United LLC (BBU). Prior to Ryan's career as a police officer, he was not a fan of law enforcement due to negative interactions with them as he was growing up. Called to the profession by God, Ryan began his professional career in 2013 by joining the Chino Police Department. Upon completing the Field Training Program, Ryan recognized the need for more transparency and dialogue between law enforcement and the community and therefore, created BBU. Since its inception, Ryan has changed the perception of many citizens, as well as police officers, throughout the world. Ryan speaks on a national level for both Law Enforcement and non-LE organizations. He has created after school programs that train and teach students about the profession of Law Enforcement and Career Development and he also has a podcast called "ITSNEEDED" which is currently downloaded in over 75 countries. Ryan began working with Dak Prescott and his non-profit, *Faith Fight Finish* in 2021 in efforts of improving the relationship between law enforcement and the youth, which has transformed the lives of many. Ryan won't cease his efforts until his goal of "Changing the face of modern-day policing" is completed. Ryan lives in Southern California with his beautiful wife and three children. Connect with Ryan at: info@breakingbarriersunited.com

Instagram: @Breaking_Barriers_United
YouTube: Breaking Barriers United
TikTok: BreakingBarriersUnited

More from ConnectEDD Publishing

Since 2015, ConnectEDD has worked to transform education by empowering educators to become better-equipped to teach, learn, and lead. What started as a small company designed to provide professional learning events for educators has grown to include a variety of services to help educators and administrators address essential challenges. ConnectEDD offers instructional and leadership coaching, professional development workshops focusing on a variety of educational topics, a roster of nationally recognized educator associates who possess hands-on knowledge and experience, educational conferences custom-designed to meet the specific needs of schools, districts, and state/national organizations, and ongoing, personalized support, both virtually and onsite. In 2020, ConnectEDD expanded to include publishing services designed to provide busy educators with books and resources consisting of practical information on a wide variety of teaching, learning, and leadership topics. Please visit us online at connecteddpublishing.com or contact us at: info@connecteddpublishing.com

Recent Publications:

Live Your Excellence: Action Guide by Jimmy Casas

Culturize: Action Guide by Jimmy Casas

Daily Inspiration for Educators: Positive Thoughts for Every Day of the Year by Jimmy Casas

Eyes on Culture: Multiply Excellence in Your School by Emily Paschall

Pause. Breathe. Flourish. Living Your Best Life as an Educator by William D. Parker

L.E.A.R.N.E.R. Finding the True, Good, and Beautiful in Education by Marita Diffenbaugh

Educator Reflection Tips Volume II: Refining Our Practice by Jami Fowler-White

Handle With Care: Managing Difficult Situations in Schools with Dignity and *Respect* by Jimmy Casas and Joy Kelly

Disruptive Thinking: Preparing Learners for Their Future by Eric Sheninger

Permission to be Great: Increasing Engagement in Your School by Dan Butler

Daily Inspiration for Educators: Positive Thoughts for Every Day of the Year, *Volume II* by Jimmy Casas

The 6 Literacy Levers: Creating a Community of Readers by Brad Gustafson

The Educator's ATLAS: Your Roadmap to Engagement by Weston Kieschnick

In This Season: Words for the Heart by Todd Nesloney, LaNesha Tabb, Tanner Olson, and Alice Lee

MORE FROM CONNECTEDD PUBLISHING

Leading with a Humble Heart: A 40-Day Devotional for Leaders by Zac Bauermaster

Recalibrate the Culture: Our Why...Our Work...Our Values by Jimmy Casas

Creating Curious Classrooms: The Beauty of Questions by Emma Chiappetta

Crafting the Culture: 45 Reflections on What Matters Most by Joe Sanfelippo and Jeffrey Zoul

Improving School Mental Health: The Thriving School Community Solution by Charle Peck and Dr. Cameron Caswell

Building Authenticity: A Blueprint for the Leader Inside You by Todd Nesloney and Tyler Cook

Connecting Through Conversation: A Playbook for Talking with Kids by Erika Bare and Tiffany Burns

The Dream Factory: Designing a Purposeful Life by Mark Trumbo

Stories Behind Stances: Creating Empathy Through Hearing "The Other Side" by Chris Singleton

Printed in the USA
CPSIA information can be obtained
at www.ICGtesting.com
JSHW011706200823
46757JS00004B/161